"I love the SBC. I've
I recognize that und
Harper and Amy Wi
the SBC easy to understand for those who want to learn more. You
should take advantage of this easy-to-read volume and enjoy!"

—**Micah Fries**, senior pastor, Brainerd Baptist Church,
Chattanooga, TN

"The Southern Baptist Convention was founded for the sake of
the Great Commission. It has always existed to facilitate churches
reaching the nations for Christ. Harper and Whitfield's new
resource provides background to our convention's history and
vision, helping us engage in the mission with our heads, our hands,
and our hearts. The question and answer format makes it an easy,
readable, and engaging resource. Every member of the SBC needs
to have this at their side."

—**J. D. Greear**, pastor, The Summit Church,
Raleigh/Durham, NC

"This book is a must read for any person that desires to know who
Southern Baptists are. It's written with knowledge and passion
about a denomination that exists to be a difference maker."

—**Johnny Hunt**, pastor, First Baptist Church
of Woodstock, GA

"Keith Harper and Amy Whitfield know Southern Baptists. They
are Southern Baptists. They know us on paper and in real interac-
tion. You can trust their answers."

—**Kevin Smith**, executive director, Baptist Convention
of Maryland/Delaware

# SBC
# FAQs

# SBC FAQs

# A Ready Reference

Keith Harper *and* Amy Whitfield

ACADEMIC

NASHVILLE, TENNESSEE

Published by B&H Academic
Nashville, Tennessee

ISBN: 978-1-4627-4843-3

Dewey Decimal Classification: 286.132

Subject Heading: SOUTHERN BAPTIST CONVENTION \
SOUTHERN BAPTISTS \ SOUTHERN BAPTIST
CHURCHES

All diagrams and graphs are courtesy of Ryan Thomas.
Images courtesy of the Southern Baptist Historical Library
and Archives, Nashville, Tennessee.

Printed in the United States of America
2 3 4 5 6 7 8 9 10 • 23 22 21 20 19 18
VP

Dedicated to Danny Akin,
whose commitment to cooperation is
an example for every Southern Baptist.

# CONTENTS

ix

# Contents

# Contents

# PREFACE

It was June 2006 when I (Amy) walked through a tunnel into the Greensboro Coliseum and first saw the Southern Baptist Convention in action. I watched in awe as a sea of paper ballots rose in the air time and again, and President Bobby Welch led 11,639 messengers through two days of actions that would affect the year to come. It was like watching a symphony. But as a new member of the orchestra, I often wondered what was happening and at times was unsure of what I was doing. I knew I had a great responsibility, and I wanted to approach it with the necessary deliberation.

After those two days, I determined to never stop learning about the processes of Southern Baptist cooperation. In the words of Aaron Sorkin (and perhaps Harry S. Truman), "Decisions are made by those who show up." But "showing up" must mean more than our mere presence. We come together to make decisions about how we will work together for the spreading of the Gospel to the ends of the earth. It must involve more than raising our hands in the air. It must involve our minds and our hearts. When we act, we should seek to understand.

This work is a compilation of questions we have asked ourselves and have heard from others over the last several years.

It is by no means exhaustive or final. New questions will arise as people continue to discover and learn. And as the Southern Baptist Convention works together in real time, answers may require adjustment or expansion. But as the conversation develops and the mission continues, this work will develop as well.

*SBC FAQs* is a ready reference for first-time messengers and longtime messengers, for students, and for church members in the pew. It is a project that began with a look in the mirror and a desire to answer the questions from over a decade ago of a young Southern Baptist who sought to understand. We truly can do more together than apart, and this is best accomplished by an informed commitment to participation. We hope our readers find answers to their questions. Even more, we hope our readers will be inspired to engage in the process of cooperation more deeply, so that together we may pursue the mission of Christ.

# PART 1
# FAQs

# What is the Southern Baptist Convention?

The Southern Baptist Convention is a body of people who are members of churches that have chosen to participate in cooperation with one another. The Convention's purpose is "to provide a general organization for Baptists in the United States and its territories for the promotion of Christian missions at home and abroad and any other objects such as Christian education, benevolent enterprises, and social services which it may deem proper and advisable for the furtherance of the Kingdom of God."[1]

## How did the Southern Baptist Convention begin?

The Southern Baptist Convention began in Augusta, Georgia, on May 8, 1845. Its stated intent was to be "for the purpose of carrying into effect the benevolent intention of our constituents by organizing a plan for eliciting, combining, and directing the energies of the denomination for the propagation of the Gospel."[2] On December 27, 1845, the General Assembly of the State of Georgia acted to incorporate the Southern Baptist Convention so that it could hold property, make its own bylaws, and participate in any business transactions. The act again stated that this was "for the purpose of eliciting, combining and directing the energies of the Baptist denomination of Christians for the propagation of the Gospel."[3]

3

The formation of the SBC was in response to the churches of the General Missionary Convention of the United States, who had struggled with the issue of slavery as the collective conscience of the nation was splitting into pieces on the eve of the Civil War. As the division between the North and the South was growing wider, the General Board faced the question of whether it was appropriate to appoint slave owners as missionaries. Pressure from both sides built until there was an unavoidable impasse. The churches of the South submitted James Reeves as a missionary candidate for consideration as a test case. They had already secured the funds for his salary from individuals in the South, so they only needed the board's approval. The General Board chose not to respond with any ruling, and in their silence there was no appointment. While they still did not articulate a direct ruling against slave owners, this nonaction spoke volumes to Southerners.[4]

The committee that met in Augusta insisted that this lack of approval was a deviation from the original intent of the General Missionary Convention, and that the requirements for missionary service were stricter than they had previously been. The Triennial Convention of the General Board had originally advocated for "the principle of a perfect equality of members, from the South and the North." Under its constitution, the standards for missionary service were full membership in a church of the denomination and full evidence of a Christian life. The committee believed that the General Board's decision (or lack thereof) amounted to a change in policy and thought that their only option was to leave the General Missionary Convention of the United States and form their own missionary-sending alliance of churches.[5]

While the churches of the Southern Baptist Convention have since expressed painful regret over the root circumstances,[6] they have also affirmed a commitment to the denomination's stated purpose, the Great Commission. Southern Baptists of the twenty-first century must necessarily acknowledge the reality of their beginnings, but they must also be ready to move forward in action with open eyes to the stated purpose for cooperation—the propagation of the Gospel.

## What is a convention, and how does it work?

A convention is one form of a deliberative assembly. It is a large group of individuals, typically serving as representatives of smaller groups, who come together at a certain appointed time to make specific decisions. It only exists at the time that it is officially called into session. *Robert's Rules of Order* defines a convention as "an assembly of delegates . . . chosen, normally for one session only, as representatives of constituent units or subdivisions of a much larger body of people in whose name the convention sits and acts."[7] In this case, the Southern Baptist Convention is composed of what it calls *messengers*, who have been sent by cooperating churches. When the messengers convene, they act as a body.

A convention only exists for a fixed amount of days, which constitute a session. In accordance with its bylaws, the Southern Baptist Convention lasts two days, currently opening on Tuesday morning and adjourning on Wednesday evening. The Committee on Order of Business will present an agenda for consideration and approval by the messengers. The agenda must include certain elements that strike a balance of inspiration and motivation to Southern Baptists with accountability and the opportunity for democratic process: a Convention sermon, the President's message, Committee reports, resolutions, and the introduction of motions.[8]

## Who are the messengers?

Messengers are those individuals who actually compose the Southern Baptist Convention at each respective meeting. The term was first used to describe delegates to associational meetings of General Baptists in England as far back as the eighteenth century,[9] and continued throughout the history of Baptists even as they formed different groups in different locations. Today, they are not delegates in the traditional sense because no authority is *delegated* to them by anyone. James L. Sullivan described them as "two way" messengers: "They go as voices of interest and concern from the churches *to* a Southern Baptist Convention. Once that Convention is over, they then become voices of communication *for* the Convention to the membership of the churches which have sent them."[10]

There are very specific parameters for who serves as a messenger to the Southern Baptist Convention. The calculation method and corresponding number of messengers has varied throughout the years, but the current practice is straightforward.

Each cooperating church may send a minimum of two messengers from their membership. Beyond those two, cooperating churches may send additional messengers according to a formula that allows for two options. One option is that for every full percent of a church's undesignated receipts in the preceding fiscal year contributed through the Cooperative Program, through the Convention's Executive Committee for Convention causes, and/or to any Convention entity, a church may send one messenger. The other option is that for every $6,000 contributed through the above channels, a church may send one messenger. Using either option, a church can send up to ten of these additional messengers, allowing for a maximum total of twelve.[11]

Messengers must provide proper credentials in one of three forms. A church can register a messenger electronically before the meeting and receive an official Southern Baptist Convention registration document. A church can provide a letter signed by the pastor, clerk, or moderator of the church that certifies the messenger's election. A messenger can also provide verification through fax, email, or some other document (electronic or physical) from their church that is deemed reliable by the Credentials Committee.[12]

Whatever form is used, it must demonstrate that a local church that meets the standards for cooperation has clearly selected the messenger.

## What determines if a church cooperates with the SBC?

Autonomy of the local church means that a church chooses to voluntarily cooperate with other churches as a part of the Southern Baptist Convention. There is no requirement to attend the annual meeting, and failure to do so does not change the status of a church. There are, however, three standards of cooperation that a church must meet in order to seat messengers.

---

### A church in friendly cooperation with the Southern Baptist Convention:

1. Has a faith and practice that closely identifies with the Convention's adopted statement of faith.
2. Has formally approved its intention to cooperate with the Southern Baptist Convention.
3. Has made undesignated financial contribution(s) through the Cooperative Program, and/or through the Convention's Executive Committee for Convention causes, and/or to any Convention entity during the fiscal year preceding.

---

1. A cooperating church has a faith and practice that closely identifies with the Baptist Faith and Message. While this phrase may seem open to interpretation, the SBC Constitution gives only one specific example. It clearly states that churches who affirm, approve, or endorse homosexual behavior would be deemed not in cooperation with the Convention.

2. A church desiring to cooperate must declare its intention to do so in some formal way. The Convention requests an annual report, and the Constitution names this as an appropriate example of this official declaration.

3. All cooperating churches must contribute financially in some way. They can do this through the Cooperative Program (which goes through their respective state conventions), through the Executive Committee to be used for Convention causes, or through a direct contribution to any entity. There is no minimum threshold for cooperation.

---

## Ways to Give:

1. Through the Cooperative Program
2. Directly through the Executive Committee to be used for Convention causes
3. To any entity

---

In the event that a church does not meet the first standard, the Convention or the Executive Committee must act to formally deem a church not in cooperation. Standards 2 and 3 are dependent on individual churches acting to declare their intentions and to contribute financially each year.[13]

# What is the relationship between the Convention and the churches?

The Southern Baptist Convention is not a hierarchical religious denomination. It is a Convention of churches that choose to cooperate with one another. This is in keeping with the Baptist distinctive of local church autonomy, and stated clearly in Article IV of the SBC Constitution: "While independent and sovereign in its own sphere, the Convention does not claim and will never attempt to exercise any authority over any other Baptist body, whether church, auxiliary organizations, associations, or Convention."[14]

Autonomous churches have complete control over their own affairs. No entity outside of those local believers has influence over that church and what it does. Hierarchy would imply that someone has authority over a congregation without being a member. The ultimate authority in a body of believers is the congregation itself.

Cooperation means that a church chooses to be in friendly relationship and to be sympathetic with the purposes and work of the Convention. It chooses to stand with all the other churches and contribute resources together toward common values and goals. Churches in friendly cooperation are those who have a faith and practice that closely identifies with the Convention's statement of faith, who have formally approved the intention to cooperate, and who have made undesignated financial contributions.

It is more appropriate to say that the relationship between the Convention and the churches is actually the relationship of the churches to the Convention. The churches support the Convention, which is composed of messengers. This means that the Convention answers to the churches, not the churches to the Convention. The autonomy of the local church is upheld in this model of the Convention carrying out the corporate wishes of the churches.

It is possible for a church to fall out of cooperating status with the Convention if it does not meet the prescribed standards. However, this does not mean that the Convention has any authority over the affairs of the local congregation. It simply means that the church no longer has a share of authority in the affairs of the Convention.

The priority of local church autonomy also means that churches are free to choose their level of participation in Convention affairs. They can send no messengers or they can send a full slate. They can engage in the cooperative process minimally by simply sending funds or more fully by their members serving on boards or committees. But it should be understood that the level of engagement determines the level to which a church has a voice in what use is made of their resources.

## Who governs the Southern Baptist Convention?

When the Convention gathers to do its business, no single messenger carries more authority or privilege than another. Every vote carries the same weight, everyone sits under the same rules, and every individual has the opportunity to use his or her voice. There are messengers who serve in specific capacities, but those roles can still be traced back to the deliberative body as a whole, either by messengers directly electing an individual to serve or by the Convention affirming a set of nominations.

The Southern Baptist Convention does not rule from the top down. Rather, it is a cooperative effort of the churches that does its business from the bottom up. The most important person in the Southern Baptist Convention is the individual messenger, and when the deliberative assembly gathers, the denomination is doing its most important work: the work that determines the future of its cooperative ministries.

## What do the messengers do when they gather?

The messengers work collectively to exercise the will of the body as a whole. However, it would be difficult for the messengers to direct every individual decision for every entity. A representative system must be employed to oversee the distribution of resources and daily operations of denominational work on behalf of the churches. This representative system happens in multiple ways.

First, the messengers elect officers—a president, a first and a second vice president, a recording secretary, and a registration secretary. There are no specific qualifications for these roles. They may be held by vocational ministers or by laypeople, by young or old, by men or women. These roles have traditionally been held by pastors, but also by state convention leaders and occasionally denominational entity leaders. Therefore, the officers are typically those who have had significant experience in vocational ministry. This demographic tendency is not dictated by any rules in the constitution or bylaws, but rather by the will of the people.

There are term limits for the office of president only, with the stipulation that the president may serve only two years consecutively. It is permissible for a former president to return to office after at least one year has passed, although this is not typical in the modern era.[15]

Messengers also approve bylaw changes and the annual operating budget, elect entity trustees as recommended by the Committee on Nominations, and any special business that arises. Trustees guide and govern entities on behalf of the Southern Baptist Convention, and the Executive Committee represents the greater body throughout the year. But the task to approve those board and committee members maintains the active role of the messengers in the Convention's governance. They trust their representatives with leadership of entities, but they do not have to do so blindly. When they raise their ballots, they are approving of the men and women who will manage their resources according to their prescribed assignments.

# What does the Southern Baptist Convention president do?

The messengers of the Convention elect a president every year to perform assigned tasks and to lead within a system of checks and balances. First, the president appoints a number of groups to serve at the annual meeting: a Committee on Committees,[16] a Committee on Resolutions,[17] a Credentials Committee to review and rule upon any questions that may arise in registration,[18] a group of tellers to tabulate votes for all elections,[19] and a team of Convention parliamentarians to assist with procedural questions.[20] Each of these groups plays a specific role in the two-day meeting, and each must be appointed every year. The president does not need Convention approval for these appointments—the approval of the Convention is given in advance when they elect the president.

Second, the president presides over the meeting itself, working with the Committee on Order of Business and the parliamentarians to ensure that all business is carried out. Leadership of the meeting is done in service to the messengers to help them carry out their will in the allotted time for each annual session. The president also would preside over any special called meetings, although that is a rare occurrence.

Third, the president serves on a number of boards and committees by virtue of the position, including entity trustee boards, the Executive Committee,[21] and the Committee on Order of Business.[22] The president of the Southern Baptist Convention also typically serves throughout the year to inspire and cast vision for the churches, as well as to represent the Southern Baptist Convention in the public eye. This often includes preaching at churches across the nation, speaking at state convention meetings and other events, meeting with government officials, and speaking to the media on behalf of the denomination. The president also serves as a fraternal messenger to the National Baptist Convention and the American Baptist Churches USA.[23]

# What is the role of the other officers of the Southern Baptist Convention?

The SBC has a first vice president and a second vice president. Vice presidents serve to assist the president in various ways. They consult with the president on appointments to the Committee on Committees, the Credentials Committee, and the Committee on Resolutions, as well as Convention parliamentarians. In the event that the president cannot serve a full term, the first vice president would take over those responsibilities, and the second vice president would take the position of first vice president. Often during the annual meeting, one or both vice presidents may preside during a session to assist the president.

The recording secretary maintains the records of the actions of the Southern Baptist Convention, which can be viewed in the *Book of Reports* and the SBC *Annual*. This person also serves on the SBC Executive Committee, and is the one who officially notifies all committee and board members of their appointments. This job is important because of the need for precise records for both legal and historical purposes.

The registration secretary supervises the Credentials Committee in reviewing any questions concerning messenger credentials, reports to the Convention the number of registered messengers, supervises tellers in the tabulation of votes, and announces election and voting results to the Convention. This role is important for ensuring integrity in all decision-making processes.

The president of the Executive Committee serves as treasurer of the Convention. This is not a position that is elected each year.

## What does the Executive Committee do?

The Executive Committee handles the administration of fiduciary decisions and governance of assets on behalf of the churches of the Southern Baptist Convention. It is a committee that essentially represents and speaks for the Convention when it is not in session.

When matters arise that an entity or agency is not already addressing, the Executive Committee acts for the Southern Baptist Convention. For example, it acts on behalf of the Convention in a legal sense with respect to transfers of property or assets. It receives all funds from the churches through the state conventions, and disburses those funds to the appropriate agencies through the Cooperative Program. It also handles all planning for the SBC Annual Meeting, recommending times and locations, making changes as necessary, and handling any contracts with cities and properties that will host the meeting.

The Executive Committee advises on questions of cooperation among entities, as well as between state conventions and national entities. It maintains the organization manual, which defines each entity's responsibilities, both to clarify duties and to protect against overlapping assignments. It also publicizes the

Southern Baptist Convention and its entities through traditional marketing avenues, as well as its news service, Baptist Press, "to interpret and publicize the overall Southern Baptist ministry."[24] The purpose of this is to tell the story of the entire picture of the Convention while supporting the work of every entity and ministry.

There is not a hierarchical relationship with any boards. The Executive Committee communicates with the trustees of entities and makes recommendations to them (as well as to the Convention as a whole), but does not have authority to control or direct any actions of those entities. Its role of communicating and recommending is important because of its perspective. Trustees of entities see the intricate details of their respective organizations. Members of the Executive Committee see the bigger picture and how all organizations are working together, and can counsel from that point of view. Ultimately, both the trustees and the Executive Committee members are accountable to the Convention as a whole. The Executive Committee maintains a regular exchange of meeting minutes with SBC entities, which helps keep this open flow of communication.

The Executive Committee proposes the operating budget of the Southern Baptist Convention and presents it to the messengers for approval each year. It also sets the format for the entities to report on their ministry plans, their financial data, and their accomplishments each year. These reports are vital for the churches to know what happens with their shared resources. Continuity in reporting is vital, and this process ensures that consistency across all agencies.[25]

# What is the difference between the SBC president and the Executive Committee president?

The president of the Southern Baptist Convention is elected by the messengers for a one-year term, with the responsibility to appoint committees and preside over deliberations when the Convention is in session. This is a voluntary position, and its duties are performed in addition to the president's daily responsibilities. The president of the Southern Baptist Convention is often a pastor, but that is not required. Entity employees have occasionally filled this role, the most recent instance being 2000–2001, when Dr. Paige Patterson served two terms as SBC president while also serving as president of Southeastern Baptist Theological Seminary. While it is rare, messengers could even elect a layperson as president.

The Executive Committee president is elected specifically by the Executive Committee for an indefinite period of time to serve in an administrative role. This individual serves as convention treasurer, manages the resources of the Convention, oversees the Cooperative Program, and maintains an office to execute daily responsibilities on behalf of the Convention. It is a full-time, salaried position, and the president manages a small staff to assist in administration.[26]

# What is the Cooperative Program?

The Cooperative Program is the Southern Baptist Convention's giving plan. An individual, a church, or a state convention may designate funds to a specific entity or effort at any time,[27] but the Cooperative Program is a way of distributing undesignated funds among the ministries of the SBC.

In the early years, the entities of the Southern Baptist Convention were each responsible for raising their own support in a societal approach to missions. Agencies campaigned for funds from the same constituencies. Overlapping financial requests led to budget deficits, which taxed the churches and the system as a whole.

After decades of this system, in 1919 the SBC launched the 75 Million Campaign to raise money for all Southern Baptist causes in one undesignated fund-raising campaign. It included all missions and ministries at both state and national levels, and received pledges from individuals and churches. The campaign did not ultimately reach its goal, leaving SBC entities in debt as pledges went unfulfilled. But in spite of the financial setback, this campaign laid the foundation for broader cooperation, and the Convention officially launched the Cooperative Program in 1925.

The Cooperative Program begins with individuals and ends with ministries. Church members give financial resources to their local congregations. Churches then forward a portion of their budget to their state convention. State conventions designate a percentage of total monies received to pass on to the Southern Baptist Convention. The messengers of each state convention decide what their respective percentages will be. Money that stays within the state is disbursed among state and local ministries.

When the Southern Baptist Convention receives funds from state conventions across the country, it immediately disburses them to SBC entities according to an established formula. Currently, that formula is:

- International Mission Board—50.41 percent
- North American Mission Board—22.79 percent
- Southern Baptist seminaries (distributed according to a formula based on full-time enrollment of Southern Baptist students)—21.92 percent
- SBC Operating Budget (managed by the Executive Committee)—2.99 percent
- Ethics and Religious Liberty Commission—1.65 percent
- Southern Baptist Historical Library and Archives—0.24 percent[28]

The Executive Committee has provided an electronic tool (http://cpcalc.sbc.net/calc/) that allows Southern Baptist churches to calculate the disbursement of their Cooperative Program donations and see how their funds will be distributed. This calculator allows anyone to choose their respective convention, enter a gift amount, and immediately see a breakdown of allocations to their state's ministries as well as to national entities.

## What is Great Commission Giving?

Great Commission Giving is a category that includes Cooperative Program contributions plus any designated funds given to Southern Baptist causes outside of the Cooperative Program. Examples of outside causes would be the Lottie Moon Christmas Offering, the Annie Armstrong Easter Offering, state missions offering, associational giving, or a designated gift to a seminary. In past years, churches reported their giving in the Annual Church Profile submitted to the Southern Baptist Convention through their respective state conventions. When a church reported only Cooperative Program giving, but had actually donated much more through designated avenues, they were unable to communicate the full extent of their giving and support for Southern Baptist missions and ministries. The call to a "Great Commission Resurgence" in 2009 and 2010 ultimately led to the establishment of this category.

While the Cooperative Program remains the primary vehicle for churches to support the SBC agencies, the category of Great Commission Giving provides a fuller way for churches to report the total amount that they give, and for the Southern Baptist Convention to honor those gifts. The Great Commission Resurgence (GCR) Task Force addressed this balance in their presentation to the 2010 Southern Baptist Convention. They affirmed the Cooperative Program and called upon Southern Baptists at every level to support it. They called on the churches to increase their giving. They called on state conventions to increase the percentage of funds they passed on to the SBC. They called upon every SBC entity to maximize their resources for the fulfillment of the Great Commission. They called on all Southern Baptists to increase their giving in every way possible—to reevaluate their budgets, to steward their wealth more, and to support the Cooperative Program like never before. But even as they spoke of increases, they also encouraged the celebration of every dollar given, including designated gifts to Southern Baptist causes.

When the task force presented its recommendations, there was discussion on the floor about how to officially prioritize the two categories. The committee worked with the messengers to amend their official recommendation, which in its final form requested the Executive Committee "to consider recommending to the Southern Baptist Convention the adoption of the language and structure of Great Commission Giving as described in this report in order to enhance and celebrate the Cooperative Program and the generous support of Southern Baptists channeled through their churches and to continue to honor and affirm the Cooperative Program as the most effective means of mobilizing our churches and extending our outreach."[29]

## How are the categories of the Cooperative Program and Great Commission Giving reported?

When churches report statistics (e.g., attendance, membership, baptisms, giving) to their local associations or state conventions, all of this data goes to the Southern Baptist Convention via LifeWay Research to compile the Annual Church Profile.

After the GCR Task Force report passed in 2010, the question remained concerning precisely how churches should prioritize their giving and then report that data.

In 2011, the Executive Committee recommended, and the Southern Baptist Convention meeting in Phoenix, Arizona, adopted that:

- The Convention respectfully request all Southern Baptist churches to make or retain the Cooperative Program as the principal component of their missions-giving strategy, and

21

- The Convention respectfully request all Southern Baptist churches strive to meet a goal of increasing their Cooperative Program gifts by 2.5 percent of undesignated gifts by the end of the 2013 calendar year, and
- The Convention respectfully request LifeWay to retain the current category and definition of "Total Mission Expenditures" in its Annual Church Profile (intended as a comprehensive category), and add a new ACP category called "Great Commission Giving," which category should only include contributions to any Baptist association, Baptist state convention, and causes and entities of the Southern Baptist Convention.[30]

## How many Southern Baptist entities are there?

There are currently eleven entities. The Southern Baptist Convention originally had two entities, the Foreign Mission Board and the Board of Domestic Missions. Over time, the Convention established boards and agencies for theological education, church resources, and public engagement. At the present time, the Southern Baptist entities are:

- International Mission Board
- North American Mission Board
- LifeWay Christian Resources
- GuideStone Financial Resources
- Southern Baptist seminaries:
  — The Southern Baptist Theological Seminary
  — Southwestern Baptist Theological Seminary

— New Orleans Baptist Theological Seminary
— Gateway Seminary of the Southern Baptist Convention
— Southeastern Baptist Theological Seminary
— Midwestern Baptist Theological Seminary
• Ethics and Religious Liberty Commission

## What is the International Mission Board?

Founded in 1845, the International Mission Board (IMB) exists to help the churches reach the world for Christ. The SBC established it under the name Foreign Mission Board with the purpose of cooperation—"one sacred effort, for the propagation of the Gospel." The IMB's stated mission is "to assist the churches of the Southern Baptist Convention to be on mission with God in penetrating the unevangelized world outside the United States and Canada with the Gospel and making Christ known among all people."[31]

While all missions and ministries of the Southern Baptist Convention are important to the churches, the International Mission Board receives the majority of funds collected through the national portion of the Cooperative Program. Christ's mandate to take the Gospel to the ends of the earth continues to be the driving force behind the support of the International Mission Board.

The IMB has four ministry assignments:

1. Assist churches by evangelizing persons, planting Baptist churches, and nurturing church planting movements among all people groups outside the United States and Canada; and, provide specialized, defined,

and agreed upon assistance to the North American Mission Board in assisting churches to reach unreached and underserved people groups within the United States and Canada.

2. Assist churches in sending and supporting Southern Baptist missionaries and volunteers by enlisting, equipping, and enabling them to fulfill their calling.

3. Assist churches and partners to mobilize Southern Baptists to be involved in international missions through praying, giving, and going.

4. Assist churches in fulfilling their international missions task by developing global strategies, including human needs–based ministries and providing leadership, administrative support, and financial accountability for implementation of these strategies.[32]

The International Mission Board is located in Richmond, Virginia. There are currently over 3,600 IMB missionaries stationed around the world.

# What is the North American Mission Board?

The North American Mission Board (NAMB) works with local associations and state conventions to reach North America with the Gospel of Christ. The organization has existed in some form since the formation of the Southern Baptist Convention. The SBC established the Board of Domestic Missions in 1845. In 1874, it became known as the Home Mission Board. In 1997, the Home Mission Board merged with the Radio and Television

Commission and the Brotherhood Commission to become the North American Mission Board.

The stated mission of the North American Mission Board is: "to work with churches, associations and state conventions in mobilizing Southern Baptists as a missional force to impact North America with the Gospel of Jesus Christ through evangelism and church planting."[33]

NAMB has six ministry assignments:

1. Assisting churches in planting healthy, multiplying, evangelistic Southern Baptist churches in the United States and Canada; and providing specialized, defined, and agreed upon assistance to the International Mission Board in assisting churches to plant churches for specific groups outside the United States and Canada.

2. Assisting churches in the ministries of evangelism and making disciples.

3. Assisting churches by appointing, supporting, and assuring accountability for missionaries serving in the United States and Canada.

4. Assisting churches by providing missions education and coordinating volunteer missions opportunities for church members.

5. Assisting churches by providing leadership development.

6. Assisting churches in relief ministries to victims of disaster and other people in need.[34]

Current major initiatives include the Send Network, a church-planting strategy with five focus regions and thirty-two Send cities; Replant, a strategy for church revitalization; God's Plan for Sharing (GPS), an evangelism initiative that aims to see

"Every Believer Sharing, Every Person Hearing" by 2020; and Send Relief, a compassion ministry to reach people "with practical help and the hope of the Gospel."[35]

The North American Mission Board is located in Alpharetta, Georgia.

## How does LifeWay Christian Resources relate to the SBC?

LifeWay Christian Resources began in 1891 as the Sunday School Board of the Southern Baptist Convention. The original charter gave it the ministry assignment of publishing Sunday school literature. LifeWay Christian Resources does not receive funds from the Cooperative Program, but does contribute financially to SBC ministries. It does, however, function as a full SBC entity. Today, its mission is: "to assist churches and believers to evangelize the world to Christ, develop believers, and grow churches by being the best provider of relevant, high quality, high value Christian products and services."[36]

LifeWay has ten ministry assignments:

1. Assist churches in the development of church ministries.
2. Assist churches in ministries to college and university students.
3. Assist churches with Christian schools and homeschool ministries.
4. Assist churches in ministries to men and women.
5. Assist churches through the operation of conference centers and camps.

6. Assist churches through the publication of books and Bibles.
7. Assist churches through the operation of LifeWay Christian Stores.
8. Assist churches through church architecture consultation and services.
9. Assist churches in capital fund-raising.
10. Assist churches by conducting research and compiling statistics.[37]

LifeWay Christian Resources is located in Nashville, Tennessee.

## How does GuideStone Financial Resources relate to the SBC?

GuideStone's stated mission from the Southern Baptist Convention is: "to assist the churches, denominational entities, and other evangelical ministry organizations by making available retirement plan services, life and health coverage, risk management programs, and personal and institutional investment programs."[38]

GuideStone has five ministry assignments:

1. Assist churches, denominational entities, and other evangelical ministry organizations by making available retirement plan programs for their ministers and employees.
2. Assist churches, denominational entities, other evangelical ministry organizations, and like-minded individuals

by making available life and health coverage and risk management programs.

3. Assist churches and denominational entities through relief to Southern Baptist ministers and Southern Baptist denominational employees.

4. Assist churches, denominational entities, other evangelical ministry organizations, and like-minded investors by making available a personal investment program to their ministers and employees and their spouses, and to like-minded investors.

5. Assist churches and denominational entities by making available institutional investment services through cooperative agreements with state Baptist foundations (or state Baptist conventions where no foundation exists) and the Southern Baptist Foundation. Assist other evangelical ministry organizations by making available institutional investment services.[39]

GuideStone Financial Resources is located in Dallas, Texas.

## What are our seminaries, and why do we have six?

There are six Southern Baptist seminaries. Originally, education was not a mission of the Convention, but soon after its establishment, many Southern Baptists wanted to provide a training option for their members in preparation for ministry. In 1859, the religion department at Furman University took steps to form The Southern Baptist Theological Seminary. The four professors who formed the first faculty—James P. Boyce, John A.

Broadus, William Williams, and Basil Manly Jr.—appealed to the Southern Baptist Convention to recognize them and provide support, as well as a governing board of trustees.[40] This began the SBC's provision of theological education.

Southern Baptists acquired or established five more seminaries over the next century—Southwestern Baptist Theological Seminary (SWBTS) in Fort Worth, Texas, in 1908; New Orleans Baptist Theological Seminary (NOBTS) in New Orleans, Louisiana, in 1917; Gateway Seminary of the Southern Baptist Convention (GS) in Mill Valley, California, in 1944; Southeastern Baptist Theological Seminary (SEBTS) in Wake Forest, North Carolina, in 1950; and Midwestern Baptist Theological Seminary (MBTS) in Kansas City, Missouri, in 1956. In 2016, Golden Gate Baptist Theological Seminary relocated to Ontario, California, and the messengers of the Southern Baptist Convention approved changing its name to Gateway Seminary of the Southern Baptist Convention (GS).

Originally, these schools largely served their respective geographic regions. Today, students select an institution for a variety of reasons, and there are signs of institutional health among all six. According to 2015–2016 data from the Association of Theological Schools, half of the top ten largest seminaries in the United States are Southern Baptist institutions.[41]

The mission for theological education in the Southern Baptist Convention is: "to prepare God-called men and women for vocational service in Baptist churches and in other Christian ministries throughout the world through programs of spiritual development, theological studies, and practical preparation in ministry."[42]

The seminaries share five ministry assignments:

1. Assist churches by programs of prebaccalaureate and baccalaureate theological education for ministers.
2. Assist churches by programs of master's level theological education for ministers.
3. Assist churches by programs of professional doctoral education for ministers.
4. Assist churches by programs of research doctoral education for ministers and theological educators.
5. Assist churches through the administration of the Southern Baptist Historical Library and Archives.[43]

Together, the leaders of all six institutions serve as the Council of Seminary Presidents, which oversees the ministries of Seminary Extension and the Southern Baptist Historical Library and Archives.

# What is the role of the Ethics and Religious Liberty Commission?

The Ethics and Religious Liberty Commission is the smallest entity of the SBC, in terms of both staff and budget.

The stated mission of the ERLC is: "to assist the churches by helping them understand the moral demands of the Gospel, to apply Christian principles to moral and social problems and questions of public policy, and to promote religious liberty in cooperation with the churches and other Southern Baptist entities."[44]

Formal attempts to engage in public policy began in earnest at the denominational level near the turn of the twentieth century. For decades, Southern Baptists worked through resolutions and appointed committees and unpaid commissions to carry out the work of both equipping and sometimes representing the churches on issues of social and civic concern.

In 1947, among the Executive Committee recommendations at the annual meeting in St. Louis was the allocation of operating budget funds for what was known at that time as the Social Service Commission.[45] In 1953, the name was changed to the Christian Life Commission.[46]

In 1997, the Executive Committee recommended that the Southern Baptist Convention change the name of the Christian Life Commission to the Ethics and Religious Liberty Commission (ERLC), with an expanded assignment that included the promotion of religious liberty.[47]

The ERLC has four ministry assignments:

1. Assist churches in applying the moral and ethical teachings of the Bible to the Christian life.
2. Assist churches through the communication and advocacy of moral and ethical concerns in the public arena.
3. Assist churches in their moral witness in local communities.
4. Assist churches and other Southern Baptist entities by promoting religious liberty.[48]

The Ethics and Religious Liberty Commission has its headquarters in Nashville, Tennessee, with additional offices in Washington, DC.

# What is the Woman's Missionary Union?

The Woman's Missionary Union (WMU) is an auxiliary of the Southern Baptist Convention, not an entity. This means that it serves as a support to the SBC, but the SBC does not govern it.

Southern Baptist women founded the WMU in 1888 to educate and support the efforts of the Foreign Mission Board and the Home Mission Board.

The WMU does not receive stated mission or ministry assignments from the SBC. However, it does set its own program statement: "Woman's Missionary Union assists churches in developing and implementing a comprehensive strategy of missions in order that a church can fulfill its total mission in the world. Woman's Missionary Union challenges Christian believers to understand and be radically involved in the mission of God."[49]

The self-designated ministries of the WMU are:

1. Assist churches in the development of Woman's Missionary Union organizations.
2. Assist churches in Christian development for women in missions.
3. Assist churches through the publication and distribution of magazines and products.[50]

The WMU also promotes a mission-style statement: "We believe in missional living. Pray for missions. Engage in mission action and witnessing. Learn about missions. Support missions. Develop spiritually toward a missions lifestyle. Participate in the work of the church and denomination."[51]

The WMU has its headquarters in Birmingham, Alabama.

# How are entities governed?

A board of trustees governs every Southern Baptist board, institution, or commission. The trustees establish bylaws, elect officers, transact business, and directly oversee the executive heads of their respective entities.

Boards have the full authority to direct the entity they are serving. The messengers gathered at the annual meeting can make requests of boards, but they cannot collectively overrule any actions taken. The Executive Committee manages ministry assignments and assists as boards work with each other in cross-agency matters, but cannot interfere in the internal affairs of a specific entity.

The messengers are, however, directly involved in the selection of all individual board members through the nomination process. When the Committee on Nominations presents its full slate of nominees, the messengers are free to debate, make amendments (substituting eligible nominees one name at a time), and register their approval through a vote. In some cases, the Convention gathered may approve or reject the removal of a trustee if requested to do so by that board (this is dependent upon the processes laid out in individual entity charters).

This maintains a system of checks and balances. The Convention cannot possibly direct the daily workings of an entity when it meets only two days a year, with thousands of messengers participating in decisions. Boards represent the messengers, and the messengers entrust the boards with management of the entities that come from the Convention's cooperation.

While the Convention cannot direct the daily actions of the trustees, it decides who can be a trustee, and it gives the power to the trustees.[52]

# What are committees, and how do they function?

The Southern Baptist Convention does its primary direct work through committees. The committees are intended to reflect the will of the messengers and to expediently carry out the business of the Convention. In addition to the Executive Committee, there are five other primary committees: the Committee on Committees, the Committee on Nominations, the Committee on Resolutions, the Committee on Order of Business, and the Credentials Committee.

The Committee on Committees meets before the annual meeting begins. This committee nominates the Committee on Nominations and any special committees that are authorized during sessions of the Convention. This committee presents its nomination report to the messengers for approval. The SBC president directly appoints the Committee on Committees, and members serve only one time.[53]

The Committee on Nominations works throughout the year to prepare its nomination report for the annual meeting. This committee is made up of two people from each qualifying state according to SBC Bylaw 30, with one of each pair being a layperson. It plays an important role, nominating the following:

1. Members of the Executive Committee of the Southern Baptist Convention
2. Directors and trustees of the boards of the Convention
3. Trustees of the institutions of the Convention
4. Trustees of the commissions of the Convention
5. Members of any standing committees (e.g., the Committee on Order of Business)

## Who Chooses Trustees?

| | |
|---|---|
| **SBC President** | Appoints Committee on Committees |
| **Committee on Committees** | Nominates Committee on Nominations |
| **Committee on Nominations** | Nominates trustees and members of standing committees |
| **Messengers** | Amend or approve report from Committee on Nominations |

Every member of the Committee on Nominations must have been a resident of his or her respective state (or affiliated with that convention) for at least three years. This is to ensure that committee members will have an informed knowledge of the people in their state for recommendation. This committee brings their report to the messengers for amendment or approval.[54]

The Committee on Resolutions proposes resolutions for consideration by the messengers. Resolutions must go through this committee in order to be processed. The committee has ten members, three of whom are members of the Executive Committee, and two of whom have served on the Committee on Resolutions the previous year. The committee receives resolutions for consideration until fifteen days before the annual meeting. They will meet immediately before the meeting to consider all submitted resolutions, and potentially to generate resolutions from within. During the annual meeting, at a pre-appointed time, the Committee on Resolutions will present its recommended resolutions to the messengers for debate and consideration. The president directly appoints this committee.[55]

The Credentials Committee serves during the annual meeting to review and rule on any questions that may arise during registration concerning the credentials of messengers. This committee serves an important role: to affirm that a church is in friendly cooperation with the Convention, and to ensure the legality of all seated messengers. The president directly appoints the Credentials Committee, which works most closely with the registration secretary.[56]

The Committee on Order of Business is a standing committee made up of the president of the Convention and six other members. The Committee on Nominations nominates it for approval by the messengers. This committee, while often unseen, plays a crucial role in the management of the two-day Convention. It prepares the agenda for the meeting, making sure that all required business is completed. Messengers vote on the proposed order of business at the beginning of each annual meeting. Once the order has been approved and the meeting begins, the Committee on Order of Business maintains the schedule, ensuring that the Convention stays on track. In the event that business takes a longer time than anticipated, the committee decides whether to recommend extending time for further debate, schedule more discussion for another session, or end the conversation. They administer the electronic microphone system that allows messengers to speak in order and ensure fairness within the rules of debate. They process all motions for disposal, advise the president on whether to schedule debate on the floor for a particular motion, refer a motion to an entity's board of trustees or the Executive Committee, or rule a motion out of order. This committee also recommends the Convention preacher for the subsequent year, as well as the Convention music director. While this committee plays a somewhat technical role, they are vital to the two days when the meeting is in session, and the messengers depend on this small group of people to make certain that the business of the Convention is accomplished. Committee members are elected for three-year terms for continuity. The Committee on Nominations brings nominees for any vacancies on the Committee on Order of Business to the messengers for their approval.[57]

# What is the role of journalism in Baptist life?

The story of Southern Baptists circulates through a number of avenues in our technological age. Originally, this took place through a network of independently owned newspapers. Many of the Baptist papers we still read today began before the founding of the Southern Baptist Convention (*Baptist and Reflector*, *Christian Index*, *Biblical Recorder*, *Western Recorder*, etc.). For decades, they functioned as independent organizations, dedicated to communicating their messages to Baptists. Today, in most cases, the state conventions support and offer a degree of oversight to the remaining papers.

The Executive Committee of the Southern Baptist Convention funds and manages Baptist Press, the official news service of the Southern Baptist Convention. The Sunday

School Board started the Southern Baptist Press Association in 1946 at the request of state convention newspaper editors. The Executive Committee then assumed responsibility for Baptist Press and in 1947 elected C. E. Bryant as director of publicity. News releases came out sporadically in the early days of Baptist Press, and then eventually they were sent out in packets with five to six stories. Today, the news service functions through a website that is updated on a continual basis. State papers reprint articles and opinion pieces as editors choose what fits their readership.

Baptist Press and the state newspapers work together to relate news about events, activities, institutions, and people. They inform Southern Baptists of trends and ongoing conversations. In addition, their archives provide researchers and historians a valuable source for information and identification. While journalists are under the oversight of the Southern Baptist Convention or respective state conventions, they continue to pursue the goal of telling stories of Baptists to Baptists in a fair and straightforward manner.[58]

# What is the relationship between the SBC and state conventions?

State conventions and the Southern Baptist Convention maintain an ongoing relationship that is based on mutual support, but without either entity having authority over the other. State conventions exist to serve the churches in their particular state or territory, and they are linked to the SBC through ministry partnerships (e.g., church planting and revitalization efforts, disaster relief, etc.).

PART 1: FAQs

In 1925, the Cooperative Program established a financial link between the two, as the most customary way to contribute to the CP is for churches to give to their state conventions. State conventions then forward a certain percentage of those funds to the Southern Baptist Convention for distribution among agencies and entities. The state conventions decide the percentages, which range from 15 to 55 percent depending on the state or territory. Most of the state conventions giving at lower percentages are outside of the Bible Belt, with small budgets and large areas to serve, in some sense having large mission fields in themselves. In recent years, there has been a movement across many state conventions to increase the percentage that goes to the SBC, but in every case, the decision is ultimately individual to each state convention.

There are forty-two Baptist conventions throughout the United States. Some territories encompass more than one state, such as the Northwest Baptist Convention or the Baptist Convention of New England. Two states, Texas and Virginia, are home to two Baptist conventions, all four of which contribute at some level to the Cooperative Program, although the Southern Baptists of Texas Convention and the Southern Baptist Conservatives of Virginia maintain a closer relationship to the SBC than the Baptist General Convention of Texas or the Baptist General Association of Virginia.

State conventions play a role in establishing regional representation on standing committees and agency boards, according to the total number of members in their churches. (Some entities also make provisions in their bylaws for local trustees, in addition to those designated through this regional representation system.)

The Southern Baptist Convention and the state Baptist conventions do not rule one another, but they depend on one another as they both serve their member churches and fuel cooperation for missions.

## What is the relationship between the SBC and local associations?

There is no formal relationship between the Southern Baptist Convention and local associations. Many churches are members of both the SBC and their local association, but this is not a necessity. Local associations exist for cooperation among churches in a specific region to serve and minister to the community around them. They often employ directors of missions (also known as associational leaders) to facilitate that work. The Southern Baptist Conference of Associational Leaders often meets during the SBC Annual Meeting, and the North American Mission Board enters into partnerships with many local associations to provide resources and reach local areas.

## What is the relationship between the SBC and other Baptist denominations?

While many existing Baptist denominations may trace similar origins, the Southern Baptist Convention possesses no formal working relationship with them. The SBC president represents Southern Baptists at the American Baptist Churches USA and National Baptist Convention annual meetings as a fraternal messenger. If he cannot attend, he may send another officer in his place. In addition, the Convention has the ability to elect fraternal messengers to any other Baptist or religious body.[59]

## In the SBC Annual Meeting, what are motions and resolutions?

According to *Robert's Rules of Order*, "A motion is a formal proposal by a member, in a meeting, that the assembly take certain action. The proposed action may be of a substantive nature, or it may express a certain view or direct that a particular investigation be conducted and the findings be reported to the assembly for possible further action, or the like."[60]

Regular motions may be made at the designated time in the order of business. Any registered messenger can make a motion. Messengers go one at a time in the order they are recognized and may only introduce a second motion if all others have finished and no one else is seeking the floor who has not made a motion during that session.

Motions must be in order, meaning that as worded they do not conflict with the charter, constitution, or bylaws of the Southern Baptist Convention. Motions that deal with the internal operations of an entity are referred to the board of that entity, in keeping with the structure of governance, to dispense with during the year. Depending on the nature of the motion, they may be automatically referred, or the Committee on Order of Business may recommend referral to the boards, to report back the following year with their responses to motions. An automatic referral would be for an issue that legally can only be handled by the trustees of an entity.

The Committee on Order of Business may choose to schedule a particular motion (necessarily excluding those that are out of order or must be automatically referred) for debate at a later time during the meeting, or the Convention may instruct the committee to do so by way of a two-thirds vote.

---

### Four things can happen to a motion:

1. Declared out of order
2. Automatic referral to agency
3. Committee recommends referral to agency
4. Discussion and vote by the messengers on the floor

---

A resolution is a specific type of motion. It is in the structure of a formal statement, typically one that is more complex than a standard motion. For this reason, resolutions must go through a lengthier process than that of simply offering a motion. Messengers submit resolutions in advance, and the Committee on Resolutions makes the official motions in their report. The Convention debates and then either approves or rejects each resolution during the precise time specified in the approved order of business. If a messenger properly submits a resolution that the Committee does not choose to recommend, the Convention may still consider it by a two-thirds vote if time has not expired in the time allowed for the committee's report. Each year, the Convention typically approves ten to twelve resolutions.

Resolutions only reflect the will of a particular Convention in a particular year. They do not speak for all of the churches of

## Resolution Order:

Messengers submit

Committee deliberates and makes recommendations

Convention amends, approves, or rejects

the Southern Baptist Convention, but rather for the majority of the messengers gathered on those two days. They are not binding on any church, association, or organization. However, these statements often have lasting public impact.

## Why do we have a business meeting every year?

When the SBC was founded in 1845, they adopted the schedule that had been followed by the Triennial Convention, meeting every three years. They only followed this for the first cycle, switching to a biennial meeting in the years leading up to the Civil War. After the Civil War, the SBC began to meet annually, a custom that continues to the present day.[61]

Article XI of the Constitution states that "the Convention shall hold its meetings annually at such time and place as it may choose." While there has been some question about the need to meet annually, most Southern Baptists have come to depend on its regularity. In 2011, the Executive Committee responded to a motion regarding the feasibility of returning to the practice of biennial meetings:

The Executive Committee reports to the Southern Baptist Convention that in its continuing efforts to be economically efficient in fulfilling its duty to "have oversight of the arrangements for the meetings of the Convention" (SBC Bylaw 18E (4)), has closely studied the fiscal implications of the possibility of returning to a pre-1866 [biennial] meeting schedule, but declines to do so for the following reasons:

- Southern Baptists are not a hierarchical group and therefore need to meet annually to discern the will of the messengers through God's leading to effectively and efficiently facilitate our cooperative mission endeavors to reach a lost and dying world with the Gospel of Jesus Christ.
- The SBC Bylaws and Business and Financial Plan require the publication and presentation of annual ministry, financial, and budgetary reports.
- Southern Baptists have always been a relational people.
- The current annual meeting schedule of the Convention enables messengers the opportunity to facilitate timely consideration and discussion of the interests of the Convention.[62]

In 2013, they responded to a similar motion:

The Executive Committee reports to the Southern Baptist Convention that it has closely studied the implications of the possibility of holding a biannual meeting and declines the recommendation in favor of our current practice of holding an annual meeting to inform

Southern Baptists about their missions and ministries, encourage them to reach the world with the Gospel of Jesus Christ, and conduct the business necessary to facilitate Southern Baptist missions and ministries.[63]

The only exception made for canceling a regular meeting is "in the case of a grave emergency," which must be decided by the Convention officers, the Executive Committee, and the executive heads of the Convention's boards and institutions acting in a body. One example of this can be seen in 1943, during the Second World War, when the Executive Committee decided to cancel the upcoming Convention. This was to cooperate with the federal government's appeal that citizens should conserve travel and transportation resources in support of the war effort.[64]

# How do states gain representation on boards and committees?

Representation on boards and committees is related to the number of members of Southern Baptist churches within each state or defined territory. According to particular thresholds, they may file an application for representation at several levels.

When a state or defined territory reaches 15,000 total members in cooperating Southern Baptist churches, an initial application may be filed for representation on the Executive Committee. Each qualified and cooperating state or defined territory automatically has a representing member of the Executive Committee. Greater representation on the Executive

Committee is in proportion to the number of total church members. This is calculated according to the following formula in SBC Bylaw 18:

Any such qualified area: One (1) Executive Committee member

250,000 church members: Two (2) Executive Committee members

500,000 church members: Three (3) Executive Committee members

750,000 church members: Four (4) Executive Committee members

1,000,000 or more church members: Five (5) Executive Committee members

Representation of one Executive Committee member is also granted to any areas that do not meet this threshold, "solely for the purpose of providing representation on the Convention's fiduciary for cooperating areas which are not yet qualified as provided above." Currently these areas are identified as the Dakotas, Iowa, Minnesota-Wisconsin and Montana.[65]

In addition, a state that reaches 15,000 total members of cooperating Southern Baptist churches may apply for representation on the Committee on Committees, and the Committee on Nominations. Once they reach 20,000 total members, they can add representation on the International Mission Board, North American Mission Board, and LifeWay. At a total of 25,000 members, they are eligible for representation on GuideStone Financial Resources, the commissions, institutions (seminaries), and standing committees.

The applications must be filed with the Executive Committee through the respective state convention president. The Executive Committee considers such requests at their February meeting and prepares them for recommendation to the Southern Baptist Convention at the annual meeting in June.[66]

## What was the Conservative Resurgence?

The Conservative Resurgence was a movement in the late twentieth century in the Southern Baptist Convention, which resulted in a shift from institutional theological progressivism to a denomination fully recommitted to a bibliocentric approach to the Christian faith.

This movement employed a grassroots political strategy whereby messengers attended the annual meeting in large numbers, actively participated in the deliberative process, and successfully elected a president who held to biblical inerrancy and committed to make appointments based on that standard. The goal was to restore committees and boards to full conservative membership, with the ultimate intention of hiring only inerrantists as entity heads. This was particularly important in Southern Baptist seminaries, where some had begun to embrace moderate and even liberal theology.

In 1989, when the majority of boards had changed and the conservatives' candidate prevailed in the eleventh consecutive presidential election, it was clear that the resurgence had been successful. The 1990s focused primarily on the changes in Southern Baptist agencies, and the movement culminated in the revision of the Baptist Faith and Message in 2000.

# What was the Great Commission Resurgence?

In the spring 2005 issue of the *Southern Baptist Journal of Theology*, Thom Rainer presented the thesis "that the conservative resurgence that began in 1979 in the Southern Baptist Convention has *not* resulted in a greater evangelistic effectiveness in the denomination."[67]

Two years later, Dr. Rainer contributed a guest column to the *Christian Post* entitled "A Plea for More Civil Discourse." In that article, he stated: "My prayer is that the conservative resurgence will now grow into a Great Commission resurgence."[68]

Daniel Akin, president of Southeastern Baptist Theological Seminary, expanded on this idea by presenting a chapel sermon entitled "Axioms of a Great Commission Resurgence."[69] This sermon called Southern Baptists to pursue denominational health, and sparked a broader conversation among churches and leaders about tangible steps the Convention could take for the future.

At the 2009 SBC Annual Meeting in Louisville, Kentucky, messengers authorized the Convention president to appoint a task force to prepare a report and recommendations "concerning how Southern Baptists can work more faithfully and effectively together in serving Christ through the Great Commission."[70] This task force brought its report to the 2010 annual meeting, and the final report as amended and adopted by the messengers included seven recommendations: the adoption of a mission statement, the adoption of core values for cooperation, requesting the Executive Committee to adopt the category of Great Commission Giving, requesting the Executive Committee to reconsider the ministry assignment of the North American Mission Board, requesting the Executive Committee to reconsider the ministry assignment of the International Mission Board, requesting the Executive Committee to work with the state conventions to develop Cooperative Program promotion and stewardship education, and requesting the Executive Committee to consider recommending an SBC Cooperative Program Allocation Budget that would increase the IMB allocation to 51 percent and decrease the Executive Committee allocation by 1 percent.

In the years since the Great Commission Resurgence Report was adopted, the SBC has fulfilled many of the recommendations, but the charge to a Great Commission Resurgence is still ongoing as Southern Baptists focus their efforts on taking the Gospel to the nations.

## Who is Lottie Moon?

The Lottie Moon Christmas Offering is well-known among Southern Baptists, as churches promote this annual opportunity to support IMB missionaries around the world. Charlotte Digges Moon, known to most as Lottie, served as a missionary to China. The Foreign Mission Board sent her in 1873 to the province of Shantung. She quickly became well-known throughout the Convention because she was devoted in her correspondence in support of mission work.

In 1887, she began urging Southern Baptist women to create an organization devoted to supporting the work of the mission boards, sparking the creation of the Woman's Missionary Union. That same year, she also suggested a special offering at

Christmas specifically for missionaries, above and beyond exist-ing support. Southern Baptist women responded, and that offer-ing continues today, with every dollar going directly to support the work of missionaries on the field. In 1918, the leaders of the WMU decided to call it the Lottie Moon Christmas Offering. It is collected in addition to the Cooperative Program, and 100 percent of monies received goes to support overseas work.

*Lottie Moon*

Lottie Moon was passionate in her devotion to the Chinese people and in her call to missions. Her story continues to capti-vate Southern Baptists today, and serves as an inspiration for the call to take the Gospel to the nations.

# Who is Annie Armstrong?

Southern Baptists are familiar with the Annie Armstrong Easter Offering that supports the North American Mission Board, but many do not know the woman for whom it is named. Annie Walker Armstrong was the first corresponding secretary for the Woman's Missionary Union, serving from 1888 to 1906. She took seriously the role of the auxiliary organization to promote missions among Southern Baptists and to advance the work of the Foreign Mission Board and the Home Mission Board. During her tenure, she was devoted to the Southern Baptist Convention and worked tirelessly to build networks among denominational entities.

*Annie Armstrong*

Armstrong stepped down from her position in 1906, but continued serving her local church. In 1934, WMU officials named the annual offering for home missions after her, and her legacy continues each spring as Southern Baptists give of themselves to support missions at home. The Annie Armstrong Easter Offering is a supplement to the Cooperative Program allocation, and 100 percent of monies received goes to support church planters and missionaries in North America.

# What is the Baptist Faith and Message?

The Baptist Faith and Message is the confessional statement for the Southern Baptist Convention. It is not required for a denomination to adopt a confessional statement, and in fact the SBC did not have one for the first eighty years of its existence. Entities had confessional statements, but not the organization as a whole.

The Convention drafted and adopted the Baptist Faith and Message in 1925 as a statement of belief in the wake of the growing influence of modernism in America. Subsequently, the statement was revised in 1963, amended in 1998, and fully revised again in 2000.

Messengers to the Convention do not have to sign the Baptist Faith and Message, and churches do not have to formally adopt it as a term of cooperation. Denominational employees are often asked to agree to it as a condition of employment, because they have been entrusted to minister on behalf of the SBC.

While the Baptist Faith and Message is not a formal standard for cooperation, it is a clear statement of position and a way that Southern Baptists communicate their core beliefs. The SBC does its work under the umbrella of that confessional statement as adopted in 2000.

# PART 2

# Guiding SBC Documents

# Southern Baptist Convention Charter[71]

## An Act to incorporate the Southern Baptist Convention.

Be it enacted by the Senate and House of Representatives of the State of Georgia, in General Assembly met, and it is hereby enacted by the authority of the same. That from and after the passing of this act, that William B. Johnson, Wilson Lumpkin, James B. Taylor, A. Docrey, R. B. C. Howell and others, their associates and successors, be and they are hereby incorporated and made a body politic by the name and style of the Southern Baptist Convention, with authority to receive, hold, possess, retain, and dispose of property, either real or personal, to sue and be sued, and to make all bylaws, rules, and regulations necessary to the transaction of their business, not inconsistent with the laws of this State or of the United States—said corporation being created for the purpose of eliciting, combining, and directing the energies of the Baptist denomination of Christians, for the propagation of the Gospel, any law, usage, or custom to the contrary not withstanding.

[Signed:]

Charles J. Jenkins

*Speaker of the House of Representatives*

Absalom H. Chappell

*President of the Senate*

Approved, December 27th, 1845

Geo. W. Crawford

*Governor*

# Southern Baptist Convention Constitution[72]

The messengers from missionary societies, churches, and other religious bodies of the Baptist denomination in various parts of the United States met in Augusta, Georgia, May 8, 1845, for the purpose of carrying into effect the benevolent intention of our constituents by organizing a plan for eliciting, combining, and directing the energies of the denomination for the propagation of the Gospel and adopted rules and fundamental principles which, as amended from time to time, are as follows:

**Article I. The Name:** The name of this body is the "Southern Baptist Convention."

**Article II. Purpose:** It is the purpose of the Convention to provide a general organization for Baptists in the United States and its territories for the promotion of Christian missions at home and abroad and any other objects such as Christian education, benevolent enterprises, and social services which it may deem proper and advisable for the furtherance of the Kingdom of God.

**Article III. Composition:** The Convention shall consist of messengers who are members of Baptist churches in cooperation with the Convention. The following subparagraphs describe the Convention's current standards and method of determining the maximum number of messengers the Convention will recognize from each cooperating church to attend the Convention's annual meeting.

1.  The Convention will only deem a church to be in friendly cooperation with the Convention, and sympathetic with its purposes and work (i.e., a "cooperating" church as that term is used in the Convention's governing documents) which:

    (1) Has a faith and practice which closely identifies with the Convention's adopted statement of faith. (By way of example, churches which act to affirm, approve, or endorse homosexual behavior would be deemed not to be in cooperation with the Convention.)

    (2) Has formally approved its intention to cooperate with the Southern Baptist Convention. (By way of example, the regular filing of the annual report requested by the Convention would be one indication of such cooperation.)

    (3) Has made undesignated, financial contribution(s) through the Cooperative Program, and/or through the Convention's Executive Committee for Convention causes, and/or to any Convention entity during the fiscal year preceding.

2. Under the terms above, the Convention will recognize to participate in its annual meeting two (2) messengers from each cooperating church, and such additional messengers as are permitted below.

3. The Convention will recognize additional messengers from a cooperating church under one of the options described below. Whichever method allows the church the greater number of messengers shall apply:

    (1) One additional messenger for each full percent of the church's undesignated receipts which the church contributed during the fiscal year preceding through the Cooperative Program, and/or through the Convention's Executive Committee for Convention causes, and/or to any Convention entity; or

    (2) One additional messenger for each $6,000 which the church contributed during the fiscal year preceding through the Cooperative Program, and/or through the Convention's Executive Committee for Convention causes, and/or to any Convention entity.

4. The messengers shall be appointed and certified by their church to the Convention, but the Convention will not recognize more than twelve (12) from any cooperating church.

5. Each messenger shall be a member of the church by which he or she is appointed.

6. If a church experiences a natural disaster or calamitous event and, as a result, the church is not qualified to appoint as many messengers as the church could appoint for the Convention's annual meeting immediately before the event, the church's pastor or an authorized church

representative may, for no more than the three (3) annual meetings after the event, certify the facts to the registration secretary and obtain the same number of messengers it could have certified for the Convention's annual meeting immediately before the event.

**Article IV. Authority:** While independent and sovereign in its own sphere, the Convention does not claim and will never attempt to exercise any authority over any other Baptist body, whether church, auxiliary organizations, associations, or convention.

## Article V. Officers:

1.  The officers of the Convention shall be a president, a first and a second vice president, a recording secretary, a registration secretary, and a treasurer.
2.  The officers shall be elected annually and shall hold office until their successors are elected and qualified. The term of office for the president is limited to two (2) years, and a president shall not be eligible for re-election until as much as one (1) year has elapsed from the time a successor is named. The first vice president shall be voted upon and elected after the election of the president has taken place; and the second vice president shall be voted upon and elected after the election of the first vice president has taken place.
3.  The president shall be a member of the several boards and of the Executive Committee.
4.  The treasurer of the Executive Committee shall be the treasurer of the Convention.

5. In case of death or disability of the president, the vice presidents shall automatically succeed to the office of president in the order of their election.

## Article VI. The Boards, Institutions, and Commissions—Their Constitution and Powers:

1. The general boards of the Convention shall be composed as follows, unless otherwise provided in their charters.

    (1) Twelve (12) members chosen from the city or vicinity of the state in which the board is located, but not more than three (3) local members elected from the same church.

    (2) One (1) member chosen from each cooperating state; and one (1) additional member from each state having two hundred and fifty thousand (250,000) members, and another additional member for each additional two hundred and fifty thousand (250,000) members in such state.

    (3) The members shall be divided into four (4) groups as nearly equal as possible, and one (1) group shall be elected each year to serve four (4) years. Board members having served two (2) full terms of four (4) years shall not be eligible for re-election until as much as two (2) years have elapsed. This shall also apply to the Executive Committee.

2. The trustees of institutions and directors shall be composed as follows:

    (1) The trustees or directors shall be elected in keeping with the requirements of the charter of the entity

as printed in the 1948 *Book of Reports* or subsequently amended with the prior approval of the Convention.

(2) If the composition of the trustees or directors is not determined by charter requirements, the body of trustees or directors shall be composed of one (1) member chosen from each cooperating state and eight (8) local members from the city or vicinity in which the entity is located, but not more than two (2) local members shall be chosen from the same church.

(3) Unless it is contrary to the charter requirements of the entity, the trustees or directors shall be divided into four (4) groups as nearly equal as possible and one (1) group shall be elected each year to serve four (4) years. Members having served two (2) full terms of four (4) years shall not be eligible for re-election until as much as two (2) years have elapsed after one has served two (2) full terms.

(4) Regardless of charter provisions, no trustee or director shall be eligible for re-election until as much as two (2) years have elapsed after the trustee or director has served two (2) full terms.

3.  Terms of Service: No trustee of a board, institution, or commission, or a member of the Executive Committee shall be eligible to serve for more than two consecutive terms. A trustee or member of the Executive Committee who has served more than half a term shall be considered to have served a full term.

4.  The governing groups of the entities may elect executive, administrative, finance, investment, and other committees if desired.

5. Each entity shall elect a president, a recording secretary, a treasurer, and such other officers as may be required. The president may be named as treasurer.

6. The compensation of its officers and employees shall be fixed by each entity, but no salaried employee or officer shall be a member of the directors of the entity.

7. Each entity is authorized to adopt its own bylaws.

8. Fifty percent of the members of the governing group shall constitute a quorum of the entity directors for transaction of any business.

**Article VII. Duties of Officers of Boards, Institutions, and Commissions:** All officers shall be subject to the control and direction of their directors in matters pertaining to the work and obligations of the board, institution, or commission. They shall perform such duties as commonly appertain to such officers.

1. The executive head of each board, institution, and commission shall be responsible to the directors for all the work of the entity and shall carry on the work as the directors may direct.

2. The recording secretary of each entity shall keep a record of all meetings of directors, if not otherwise provided for, and shall keep the records in fireproof safes, vaults, or files.

3. The treasurer of each entity shall follow approved methods of accounting, keep the books, receipt for all monies and securities, deposit all funds with a depository or depositories approved by the directors, and render

full statements as required to the directors or to the Convention. The treasurer shall not pay out money except as the directors may order and direct.

**Article VIII. Church Membership:** Officers of the Convention, all officers and members of all boards, trustees of institutions, directors, all committee members, and all missionaries of the Convention appointed by its boards shall be members of Baptist churches cooperating with this Convention.

**Article IX. Missionaries' Qualifications:** All missionaries appointed by the Convention's boards must, previous to their appointment, furnish evidence of piety, zeal for the Master's Kingdom, conviction of truth as held by Baptists, and talents for missionary service.

**Article X. Distribution of Funds:** The Convention shall have the right to designate only undesignated funds, the right of contributors to the work of the Convention to designate the objects to which their contributions shall be applied being fully recognized.

## Article XI. Meetings:

1. The Convention shall hold its meetings annually at such time and place as it may choose.
2. The president may call special meetings with the concurrence of the other officers of the Convention and of the Executive Committee.
3. The Executive Committee may change the time and place of meeting if the entertaining city withdraws its invitation or is unable to fulfill its commitments.

4. The Convention officers, the Executive Committee, and the executive heads of the Convention's boards and institutions acting in a body may, in case of grave emergency, cancel a regular meeting or change the place of meeting.

**Article XII. As to Conflict with State Laws:** All incorporated entities of the Convention shall be required to comply with the letter and spirit of this Constitution, the Bylaws, and the Business and Financial Plan insofar as they are not in conflict with the statute law of the state in which an entity is incorporated, and nothing herein contained shall be construed to require any such incorporated entity to act and carry on its affairs in conflict with the law of the state of its incorporation. In case any action of any entity of the Convention is found to be a violation of the law of the state of its incorporation, said action shall be reported by that entity to the Convention for appropriate action.

**Article XIII. Definition of a State:** The District of Columbia shall be regarded as a state for the purpose of this Constitution, the Bylaws, and all actions of the Convention.

**Article XIV. Amendments:** Any alterations may be made in these Articles at any annual meeting of the Convention by a vote of two-thirds of the messengers present and voting at the time the vote is taken, provided that an amendment shall be so approved by two (2) consecutive annual meetings of the Convention.

# Southern Baptist Convention Bylaws[73]

In order to carry out the provisions of the Constitution, the following Bylaws are adopted for the government of the Convention:

1. **Convention Session:**
    A. The Convention shall open with the Tuesday morning session and continue through Wednesday, holding such sessions as the Committee on Order of Business finds necessary for the conduct of business, except that sufficient time on Wednesday afternoon shall be reserved for seminary luncheons and other necessary meetings.

    B. The Convention sermon and president's message shall be considered as fixed orders at the time designated by the committee on Order of Business.

    C. A messenger may speak in debate for longer than three minutes only with the permission of the Convention granted by a two-thirds vote.

    D. A messenger may introduce a second motion during a business session only if no other messenger is seeking the floor who has not made a motion during that session.

2. **Presentation of Outside Causes:** Causes other than those provided for in the regular work of the Convention may be presented to the Convention upon authority of officers of the Convention in conference with the Committee on Order of Business in such ways and at such times as may be dictated by the courtesies of the case and the necessities of the program.

3. **Convention Site:**

   A. No city shall be considered as a meeting place for the Southern Baptist Convention in which there is a considerable distance between the available hotels and the Convention hall.

   B. No meetings other than the Convention services shall be held in the Convention hall during the sessions of the Convention. Every service held in the Convention auditorium shall be under the direction of the Committee on Order of Business.

4. **Exhibits:** All exhibits of every description shall be rigidly excluded from those parts of the place of meeting where the people visiting the exhibits will disturb the proceedings of the Convention, their locations to be determined by the Executive Committee or its agent. The Executive Committee of the Convention shall have exclusive control of all exhibit space.

5. **Book of Reports:**

   A. Copy for reports and recommendations to the Convention shall be submitted to the recording secretary by March 1, unless circumstances beyond the control of the reporting entity or committee make it impossible.

B. Recommendations of entities and committees of the Convention may not be voted upon until the recommendations have been printed in the *Book of Reports* or the Convention *Bulletin*. The recording secretary is authorized to provide the Baptist Press and other interested parties, upon their request, copies of recommendations requiring Convention action.

6. **Convention Annual:** The Convention *Annual* containing reports and actions of the Convention and other pertinent material shall be published as soon as possible after the meeting of the Convention and shall be made available without charge to all active pastors and denominational agents.

7. **Bulletin:**

A. The Executive Committee of the Convention shall have printed each day a sufficient number of brief reports, or bulletins, of the Journal of Proceedings, reporting specifically matters of business proposed and acted upon, including the names of committees appointed, reports of the committees, and such business as may be transacted and carried over to the following day, also including a list of the titles or subjects of the resolutions presented and the names of the persons presenting them.

B. Such report, or bulletin, shall not include speeches or addresses or any comment thereon, a photograph, or any personal reference to any messenger of the Convention, but shall be only a resume of the business transacted during that day.

8. **Messenger Credentials and Registration:**

A. Each person elected by a church cooperating with the Southern Baptist Convention as a messenger to the Southern Baptist Convention shall be registered as a messenger to the Convention upon presentation of proper credentials. Credentials shall be presented by each messenger, in person, at the Convention registration desk and shall be in the following form:

(1) A completed, properly authorized, official Southern Baptist Convention registration document, certifying the messenger's election in accordance with Article III. Composition, of the Constitution of the Southern Baptist Convention; but if the messenger does not have the messenger registration document,

(2) A letter from the messenger's church, signed by the pastor, clerk or moderator of the church, certifying the messenger's election in accordance with Article III. Composition, of the Constitution of the Southern Baptist Convention; or

(3) Some other document (which may include a fax, email, or other physical or electronically transmitted document) from the messenger's church which is deemed reliable by the Credentials Committee or qualifies under guidelines approved by the registration secretary and the Credentials Committee.

Messengers registered in accordance with this section shall constitute the Convention.

B. The president of the Convention, in consultation with the vice presidents, shall appoint, at least thirty (30) days before the annual session, a Credentials Committee to serve at the forthcoming sessions of the Convention. This committee shall review and rule upon any questions which may arise in registration concerning the credentials of messengers. Any such ruling may be appealed to the Convention during business session. Any contention arising on the floor concerning seating of messengers shall be referred to the committee for consideration and the committee shall report back to the Convention.

C. The registration secretary shall be at the place of the annual meeting at least one (1) day prior to the convening of the first session of the Southern Baptist Convention for the purpose of opening the registration desk and registering messengers. The registration secretary also shall convene the Credentials Committee at least one day prior to the annual meeting and shall assist the committee in reviewing questions concerning messenger credentials. The registration secretary shall report to the Convention the number of registered messengers.

9. **Address of Welcome:** There may be one (1) address of welcome limited to ten (10) minutes and one (1) response thereto limited to ten (10) minutes.

10. **Election of Officers and Voting:**
    A. The president, the first and second vice presidents, and the secretaries shall be elected at the Convention, their terms of office to begin at the final adjournment.
    B. Election of officers shall be by ballot, provided however that if there is only one (1) nomination, and no other person desires to nominate, the secretary or anyone designated for the purpose may cast the ballot of the Convention. If an officer does not receive a majority of votes cast on the first ballot, subsequent ballots shall carry the names of those who are included in the top 50 percent of the total votes cast in the previous ballot.
    C. Nominating speeches for officers of the Convention shall be limited to one (1) address of not more than three (3) minutes for each nominee.
    D. The president, in consultation with the registration secretary, shall appoint tellers. The tabulation of any vote by the tellers or otherwise (such as by electronic means) shall be under the supervision of the registration secretary. The president or registration secretary shall announce election and voting results to the Convention as soon as practicable.
    E. Any materials, instructions, and/or devices necessary to vote shall be made available to the messengers.
    F. No proxy voting is permitted. All propositions, decisions, and choices shall be by a majority vote of the messengers present and voting in person, except where provisions have been made for a greater than

majority vote. Except for officer elections, votes may be taken by ballot, by voice, by rising, by show of hands, by common consent, or by some other acceptable method. "Ballot" shall include electronic voting that protects the integrity of the voting process and provides for messengers' votes to remain confidential.

11. **Parliamentary Authority and Parliamentarians:** The parliamentary authority of the Southern Baptist Convention shall be Robert's Rules of Order (latest revised edition). The Convention president, in conference with the vice presidents, shall select a chief parliamentarian and assistant parliamentarians, as necessary, to advise the presiding officers of the Convention on matters of parliamentary procedure. The chief parliamentarian shall be a person of experience and knowledge, sufficient to qualify him or her to serve as parliamentarian to the Southern Baptist Convention, and he or she shall be certified by the American Institute of Parliamentarians and/or the National Association of Parliamentarians. It shall be the responsibility of the president and treasurer of the Executive Committee of the Southern Baptist Convention to sign, on behalf of the Executive Committee, any contracts or letters of agreement related to the services of the chief parliamentarian.

12. **Ministry Leaders:** Leaders of Southern Baptist Convention entities shall be admitted to the Convention sessions and shall be authorized to serve as resource persons for discussion of those matters which affect their areas of ministry responsibility.

13. **Memorial Services:** The Committee on Order of Business is instructed to arrange for any memorial service to be held during the Convention.

14. **Entities and Auxiliary of the Convention:**

   A. The entities of the Convention are as follows:

   (1) General Boards: The International Mission Board of the Southern Baptist Convention, Richmond, Virginia; The North American Mission Board of the Southern Baptist Convention, Inc., Alpharetta, Georgia; LifeWay Christian Resources of the Southern Baptist Convention, Nashville, Tennessee; GuideStone Financial Resources of the Southern Baptist Convention, Dallas, Texas.

   (2) Institutions: The Southern Baptist Theological Seminary, Louisville, Kentucky; The Southwestern Baptist Theological Seminary, Fort Worth, Texas; New Orleans Baptist Theological Seminary, New Orleans, Louisiana; Gateway Seminary of the Southern Baptist Convention, Ontario, California; The Southeastern Baptist Theological Seminary, Inc., Wake Forest, North Carolina; Midwestern Baptist Theological Seminary, Inc., Kansas City, Missouri.

   (3) Commission: The Ethics and Religious Liberty Commission of the Southern Baptist Convention, Nashville, Tennessee.

   B. Auxiliary: Woman's Missionary Union, Birmingham, Alabama, is an auxiliary of the Convention.

15. **Committee on Nominations:**

   A.  The Committee on Nominations shall be composed of
       two (2) members from each qualified state, who shall be
       elected by the Convention. Nominations for each posi-
       tion shall be made by the Committee on Committees.
       The Committee on Committees shall make its recom-
       mendation of nominees to the Convention in the form
       of a single motion to elect all those persons it recom-
       mends for the Committee on Nominations. The motion
       may be amended but no messenger shall be allowed to
       propose more than one (1) person at a time for election.
       When adopted by the Convention, the motion of the
       Committee on Committees, as amended, shall consti-
       tute the election of the persons named in the motion
       to the Committee on Nominations. One (1) person
       nominated to the Committee on Nominations from
       each state shall be a person not employed full time by
       (or retired from) a church or denominational entity.
       Persons nominated to the Committee on Nominations
       shall have been resident members for at least three (3)
       years of Southern Baptist churches either geographi-
       cally within the states or affiliated with the conventions
       of the states from which they are elected.

   B.  The Committee on Nominations thus elected shall
       prepare its report through the year, carefully follow-
       ing the provisions of the Constitution and Bylaws of
       the Convention and the documents of the respec-
       tive Convention entities, and shall recommend to
       the next Convention the following:

(1) Members of the Executive Committee of the Southern Baptist Convention

(2) Directors/trustees of the boards of the Convention

(3) Trustees of the institutions of the Convention

(4) Trustees of the commissions of the Convention

(5) Members of any standing committees

C. Excluding the president and recording secretary of the Convention, and the president of Woman's Missionary Union, and unless otherwise specifically permitted or required by these bylaws, no person shall be eligible to be elected or appointed to serve simultaneously on more than one of the boards, institutions, commissions, or committees of the Convention, or as a member of the Executive Committee, and no person shall be elected or appointed to serve on one of these bodies if that person's spouse has been elected or appointed to serve on one of these bodies for a time which would be simultaneous.

D. The committee shall not recommend a fellow committee member or the member's spouse or a member of the previous year's Committee on Committees or the member's spouse for a first term on an entity.

E. The committee shall recognize the principle that the persons it recommends shall represent the constituency of the Convention, rather than the staff of the entity.

F. No person and no person's spouse shall be eligible to serve on the board of any one of the above entities (1) from which the person receives, directly or indirectly, any form of payment or financial benefit except for reimbursements for reasonable and authorized expenses incurred in the performance of the duties of a trustee, or, (2) which provides funds for which he/she has a duty of administration. When such conditions become applicable, that person or that person's spouse shall be considered as having resigned and such vacancy shall be filled in accordance with established Convention procedure.

G. All of the above entities shall include both church or denominational employees and those who are not church or denominational employees. Not more than two-thirds of the members of any of these entities shall be drawn from either category. Where a person was serving as a church or denominational employee at the time of retirement, he/she should be counted as a church or denominational employee after retirement as far as the work of the Committee on Nominations is concerned.

H. Any person elected to serve on any of the boards, institutions, commissions, or the Executive Committee, shall at the time of such election have been continuously a resident member for at least the preceding three (3) years of a church or churches which were in those years in friendly cooperation with the Convention and sympathetic with its purposes and work, and, where representation is by qualifying states, which were either geographically within the state or affiliated with the convention of the state from which the person is elected. Any person who is a member of one of these entities shall be considered as having resigned when the person ceases to be a resident member of a church either geographically within the state or affiliated with the convention of the state from which he/she has been elected as a representative.

I.  No person who has served on the board of an entity or on the Executive Committee shall be eligible to serve on the board of any entity or on the Executive Committee until two years after the conclusion of his or her term of office, except that a person may be re-elected to an authorized successive term or serve by virtue of a separate office.

J.  The report of the Committee on Nominations shall be released to Baptist Press no later than 45 days prior to the annual meeting of the Convention and shall be published in the first day's *Bulletin*. Persons desiring to amend the report of the Committee on Nominations are encouraged to publicize the nature of their amendment sufficiently in advance of the annual meeting of the Convention to allow information concerning the amendment to be made available to Convention messengers.

K.  The Committee on Nominations shall make its recommendation to the Convention in the form of a motion to elect those persons it recommends for specific terms of office. The motion may be amended but no messenger shall be allowed to propose more than one (1) person at a time for election. When adopted by the Convention, the motion of the Committee on Nominations, as amended, shall constitute the election of the persons named in the motion to their respective terms of office.

16. **Vacancies on Boards:** All entities shall report all vacancies on the entities to the Committee on Nominations immediately on the occurrence of such vacancies. Any entity's board may make interim appointments only when authorized by its charter. Any such appointment shall only be of a person who is eligible and qualified both to be elected by the Convention and to serve according to the Constitution and Bylaws of the Southern Baptist Convention.

17. **Fraternal Messengers:**

   A. The Convention shall send a fraternal messenger to the annual sessions of the American Baptist Churches and the National Baptist conventions. The expenses of the fraternal messengers incurred while in attendance upon the conventions herein named shall be included in the items of Convention expenses.

   B. The fraternal messenger to the American Baptist Churches shall be the president of the Southern Baptist Convention at the time of the meeting of the American Baptist Churches, and he shall also be the fraternal messenger to the other National Baptist conventions named. If the president is unable to attend, he shall be authorized to name another officer as a substitute.

C. The fraternal messengers to other Baptist bodies or other religious bodies may be elected by the Convention as occasion may require. The expenses of such messengers shall be borne by the messengers themselves unless specifically provided for by the Convention.

18. **The Executive Committee:**

A. The Executive Committee shall consist of the president and the recording secretary of the Convention, the president of the Woman's Missionary Union, and one (1) or more members from each qualified and cooperating state or defined territory of the Convention, subject to the provisions of Section 30 of the Bylaws.

(1) Once the number of members of cooperating Southern Baptist churches in such an area reaches the levels shown in the following table, the number of Executive Committee members from that area shall thereafter be as indicated:

Any such qualified area: One (1) Executive Committee member

250,000 church members: Two (2) Executive Committee members

500,000 church members: Three (3) Executive Committee members

750,000 church members: Four (4) Executive Committee members

1,000,000 or more church members: Five (5) Executive Committee members.

(2) In addition, and solely for the purpose of providing representation on the Convention's fiduciary for cooperating areas which are not yet qualified as provided above, there shall be one Executive Committee member from each of the four following geographical areas: the Dakotas, Iowa, Minnesota-Wisconsin, and Montana.

(3) Except for areas represented by only one member, at least one-third of the members from any area shall be persons employed by a church or denominational entity, and at least one-third of the members from that area shall be persons not employed by a church or denominational entity.

(4) At least one-third of the entire membership of the Executive Committee shall be persons employed by a church or denominational entity, and at least one-third of its members shall be persons not employed by a church or denominational entity.

(5) Except for the president and the recording secretary of the Convention and the president of Woman's Missionary Union, the following persons are disqualified from serving as members of the Executive Committee:

a. Employees of the Convention or its Executive Committee

b. Trustees, directors, or employees of a Convention entity or its auxiliary

c. Employees of a convention for a state or defined territory, or of an entity or body that is empowered to act on behalf of such a convention

    d.   Employees of an entity of a convention for a state or defined territory

B.  Members shall be divided into four (4) groups as nearly equal as possible and shall hold office for four (4) years, one-fourth going out of office each year.

C.  A majority of the Committee shall constitute a quorum.

D.  The Executive Committee shall elect a president, who shall also be treasurer, and other officers and staff who may be needed. All the main executive officers and all the office employees who handle funds shall be bonded, and no salaried officer or employee shall be a member of the Executive Committee

E.  The Executive Committee shall be the fiduciary, the fiscal, and the executive entity of the Convention in all its affairs not specifically committed to some other board or entity.

The Executive Committee is specifically authorized, instructed, and commissioned to perform the following functions:

(1) To act for the Convention ad interim in all matters not otherwise provided for.

(2) To be named in transfers of real and personal property for the use and benefit of the Convention either by deed, conveyance, will, or otherwise and to affix the seal of the Convention to all approved

transactions; and to take title to and hold or to convey title to all properties, real or personal, and all funds, monies, and securities that are donated or transferred or left by will to or for the use of the Convention. As to such properties, funds, monies, and securities as the Executive Committee shall hold and not convey title to, the Executive Committee shall be custodian of such, holding them in trust for the Convention to be managed, controlled, and administered by the Executive Committee in accordance with the direction, general or specific, of the Convention. Rules governing the handling of securities set out in Article VII, Section 3, of the Constitution shall be observed by the Executive Committee.

(3) To receive and receipt for all current funds of the Convention including all undesignated cooperative missionary, educational, and benevolent funds and all current special or designated funds for missionary, educational, and benevolent purposes which may be contributed by individuals, churches, societies, corporations, associations, or state conventions; and to disburse all undesignated funds, according to the percentages fixed by the Convention and all the designated funds according to the stipulations of the donors. The Executive Committee shall keep the accounts of all inter-entity groups and shall disburse their funds on requisition of the properly constituted officers of the inter-entity organization.

(4) To recommend to the Convention a time and place and to have oversight of the arrangements

for the meetings of the Convention, with authority to change both the time and place of the meetings in accordance with the provisions of Article XI, Section 3, of the Constitution.

(5) To act in an advisory capacity on all questions of cooperation among the different entities of the Convention, and among the entities of the Convention and those of other conventions, whether state or national.

(6) To present to the Convention each year a consolidated and comprehensive financial statement of the Convention and all its entities, which statement shall show the assets and liabilities of the Convention and all its entities, and all the cash and other receipts of the year.

(7) To present to the Convention a comprehensive budget for the Convention and for all its entities, which budget shall include the budgets of all the entities of the Convention whether or not they receive Cooperative Program funds, as reviewed by the Executive Committee. The Executive Committee shall recommend the amount of Convention funds which may be allocated to each cause. It shall not recommend any direct allocation of funds for any entity or institution for which the Convention does not elect trustees or directors.

(8) To conduct the general work of promotion and the general work of publicity for the

Convention in cooperation with the entities of the Convention. The Executive Committee shall provide a Convention relations service and a Convention news service to interpret and publicize the overall Southern Baptist ministry. These services shall be available to support the work of all Convention entities and ministries.

(9) To maintain open channels of communication between the Executive Committee and the trustees of the entities of the Convention, to study and make recommendations to entities concerning adjustments required by ministry statements or by established Convention policies and practices, and, whenever deemed advisable, to make recommendations to the Convention. The Executive Committee shall not have authority to control or direct the several boards, entities, and institutions of the Convention. This is the responsibility of trustees elected by the Convention and accountable directly to the Convention.

(10) To make its own bylaws in keeping with the Constitution and Bylaws of the Convention in carrying out these instructions to the Executive Committee; to hold meetings whenever deemed necessary; to make reports of all meetings to the Convention; to notify all the boards, entities, and institutions of the actions of the Convention and to advise with them as to the best way of promoting all the interests of the Convention.

(11) To derive, in accordance with the action of the Convention in Atlanta in 1944, the expenses of the Executive Committee from the Operating Budget of the Convention specifically established for this purpose and formally approved by the Convention.

(12) To utilize an appropriate report format which will enable the Executive Committee to obtain from the entities adequate and comparable information about ministry plans, accomplishments, and financial data.

(13) To maintain an official organization manual defining the responsibilities of each entity of the Convention for conducting specific ministries and for performing other functions. The manual shall cite the actions of the Convention that assigned the ministries and other functions to the entity. The Executive Committee shall present to the Convention recommendations required to clarify the responsibilities of the entities for ministries and other functions, to eliminate overlapping assignments of responsibility, and to authorize the assignment of new responsibilities for ministries or functions to entities.

(14) To send copies of the minutes of the Executive Committee to the heads of all Southern Baptist Convention entities, and copies of the minutes of all entities shall be sent to the office of the Executive Committee.

19. **Committee on Committees:** A Committee on Committees, composed of two (2) members from each

qualified state and the District of Columbia, shall be appointed by the president, in conference with the vice presidents, of whom one (1) shall be designated as chairperson. Persons named to the Committee on Committees shall have been resident members for at least three (3) years of Southern Baptist churches either geographically within the states or affiliated with the conventions of the states from which they are appointed. Members so named shall be notified by the president in writing, at least 45 days before the meeting of the Convention. Their names shall be released by the president to Baptist Press no later than 45 days prior to the annual meeting of the Convention, and their names shall be published in the first issue of the Convention *Bulletin*. The president may fill any vacancies on the committee when those originally named do not attend the Convention. This committee shall nominate all special committees authorized during the sessions of the Convention not otherwise provided for. All special Convention committees shall transfer, upon their discharge, all official files to the Executive Committee of the Southern Baptist Convention.

20. **Committee on Resolutions:** At least seventy-five (75) days in advance of the Convention, the president, in conference with the vice presidents, shall appoint a Committee on Resolutions to consist of ten (10) members, any two (2) of whom shall have served as Committee on Resolutions members during the prior year, and any three (3) of whom shall be members of the Executive Committee. One of the Committee members

shall be designated as chairperson. Members so named shall be notified by the president in writing at least 75 days before the annual meeting of the Convention. The names of the members of the Committee on Resolutions shall be released by the president to Baptist Press no later than 75 days prior to the annual meeting of the Convention, and their names shall be published in the first issue of the Convention *Bulletin*.

In order to facilitate thorough consideration and to expedite the Committee's work, all proposed resolutions shall:

1) Be submitted to the Committee for review and consideration as early as April 15th, but no later than fifteen (15) days prior to the next SBC annual meeting,

2) Be addressed to the Committee on Resolutions in care of the Executive Committee of the Southern Baptist Convention at its registered or e-mail address (electronic copies are preferred),

3) Be typewritten, titled, and dated,

4) Be accompanied by a letter from a church qualified to send a messenger to the annual meeting of the Southern Baptist Convention certifying that the person submitting the resolution is a member in good standing, and

5) Include complete contact information for both the person submitting it, and his or her church.

No person may submit more than three resolutions per year. The Committee on Resolutions shall prepare and submit to each annual meeting of the Convention only such resolutions the Committee recommends for adoption. Such resolutions may be based upon proposals received by the Committee or may originate with the Committee. Only resolutions recommended by the Committee may be considered by the Convention, except the Convention may, by a 2/3 vote, consider any other resolution properly submitted to the Committee.

A list of the titles of all properly submitted proposed resolutions shall be printed in the Convention *Bulletin*. The list shall include the name and city of each person properly submitting a resolution, and the disposition of each proper submission.

21. **Committee on Order of Business:** The Committee on Order of Business, a standing committee, shall consist of seven (7) members—the president of the Convention and six (6) other members, two (2) of whom shall be elected each year for a term of three (3) years and two (2) of whom shall be persons not employed full time by a church or denominational entity. No member of the committee can succeed himself or herself. The committee shall suggest an order of business for the next meeting of the Convention. It shall provide periods of time during the Convention for the introduction of all matters requiring a vote not scheduled on the agenda, and, when introduced (unless the Convention then gives its unanimous consent for its immediate consideration) shall fix times for the consideration of the same. All such matters of business shall be introduced to the Convention by the end of the afternoon session of the first day of the annual meeting of the Convention. When practicable it

shall give notice in the Convention *Bulletin* of the substance of the motion or resolution and the time for its consideration. If unable to give notice in the *Bulletin*, it shall cause announcement to be made from the floor of the Convention of the same, action thereon to be taken at the subsequent session of that Convention. The committee shall recommend to the Convention a preacher for the succeeding Convention sermon and the director of music. The director of music shall be elected annually and the term of office is limited to two (2) years. The director of music shall not be eligible for re-election until as much as one (1) year has elapsed from the time a successor is named.

22. **Notification of Committees:** Within thirty (30) days after the Convention adjourns, the recording secretary shall notify the members of all committees of their appointment and all chairpersons of their position and furnish each one a list of that committee. The recording secretary shall also notify all board members, trustees of institutions, and commission members of their appointment.

23. **The Great Commission Council:** The Great Commission Council shall serve as the organization through which the various entities and the auxiliary of the Convention will correlate their work. The membership of the Great Commission Council shall be composed of the chief executives of The Executive Committee of the Southern Baptist Convention, the auxiliary of the Convention, and the entities named in Bylaw 14.

A. The work of the Council shall be in keeping with its prescribed functions. It will neither launch nor execute ministries; it will formulate no policies, except those which govern its own activities. Its chief purpose is that of consultation, communication, and cooperation. The scope of its work will be that of:

(1) finding ways of mutual re-enforcement in assigned responsibilities and distinctive ministries;

(2) considering and seeking to avoid overlapping endeavors and competitive ministries;

(3) considering the means for helping the churches fulfill their divine mission in Bible teaching, evangelism, world missions, stewardship, Christian training, education, and Christian social service;

(4) finding ways for effective cooperation in promoting the total work of the Southern Baptist Convention;

(5) considering the significant factors affecting the work and witness of the denomination; and

(6) seeking to find the means through which the power of the Christian Gospel may be comprehensively and effectively applied to the ends of the earth.

B. In the matter of relationships:

(1) the Council is not, itself, an entity of the Convention;

(2) it has no authority over the several entities;

**91**

(3) its decisions are not binding on the entities, since the boards and commissions must retain the authority to reach the decisions required to carry out their own responsibilities;

(4) its relationship to the entities is purely advisory;

(5) the Council does not report formally either to the Convention or the Executive Committee, nor does the Convention refer matters directly to the Great Commission Council;

(6) it may receive from and refer to the Executive Committee problems for consideration;

(7) it is not required to take formal action with regard to matters referred to it by the Executive Committee in serving as a channel of cooperation and correlation relative to the work of the Convention; and

(8) the Council sustains no direct relationship with state conventions or local churches, but it will strive to be mindful of the needs of the churches as well as the functions and ministries of the several conventions.

24. **Ministry Statements:** The ministry statements of the entities as approved by the Southern Baptist Convention and published in the 1967 *Annual* and subsequently amended, renamed, or rewritten, and approved by the Convention, express the policy of the Convention with respect to the ministries of the entities of the Convention.

25. **New Enterprises and Abolishing of Entities:** No new enterprise, involving expenditure of money, shall be authorized by the Convention except upon favorable action by the Convention in two (2) succeeding annual meetings; provided, however, that this restriction shall not apply to a recommendation of an entity of the Convention concerning its own work. No entity shall be discontinued without a majority vote at two (2) successive annual sessions of the Convention.

26. **Procedures:**

   A. *Method of Procedure for Entities:* To facilitate consideration and discussion of the interests of the Convention, the following method of procedure is hereby adopted:

   (1) Printed reports of the boards, institutions, commissions, and standing committees shall be consolidated into the *Book of Reports* for distribution to messengers on their enrollment;

   (2) Reports of all special commissions and standing committees, containing recommendations for the Convention's action, shall be included in the *Book of Reports*; and

   (3) All recommendations of each board, institution, commission, special committee, and standing committee shall be printed together at the end of its report before they may be considered by the Convention. In case any entity or committee shall be unable to comply with this requirement, its recommendation shall be printed in the Convention

*Bulletin* before consideration and action by the Convention. Recommendations by an entity which are not published in the *Book of Reports* or the Convention *Bulletin* shall, when presented to the Convention, be referred to the Executive Committee or to such other committee as the Convention may direct.

B. *Procedure for Motions of Messengers Concerning Entities:* Motions made by messengers dealing with internal operations or ministries of an entity shall be referred to the elected board of the entity for consideration and report to the constituency and to the next annual meeting of the Convention for action with the exception that the Committee on Order of Business may be instructed by a two-thirds vote to arrange for consideration at a subsequent session of the same Convention, subject to provision of Bylaw 21.

On all matters referred by the Convention, entities shall respond in writing at the close of their report in the *Book of Reports* and *Annual,* giving specific information on:

(1) how the matter referred was considered;

(2) how it was reported to the constituency; and

(3) any actions on the matter taken by the entity or action proposed to the Convention.

C. *Limitations:* The last one-third of the time allotted for consideration of every entity report before the Convention shall be reserved for discussion from the floor.

27. **Publicity and Press Representative:**

    A. Boards, institutions, and special committees dealing with matters of general importance and interest shall have in the hands of the press representative of the Convention, at least one (1) week in advance, copies of digests of their report to be submitted to the approaching Convention.

    B. The press representative shall cooperate with the representatives of the secular press in furnishing intelligent, accurate, and creditable reports of this Convention while in session.

28. **Closing of Books:** Entities of the Convention shall close their books and accounts and have them audited as of midnight September 30, or in the case of the seminaries, July 31, or in the case of GuideStone Financial Resources, December 31. Supplemental reports for the period between the closing of the books of the entities and the Convention session should be included in the reports to the Convention.

29. **Participation in Convention Affairs:** To allow participation in the affairs of the Convention, any member of a church who is eligible to be a messenger to the Convention may be appointed teller, a member of the Credentials Committee, a member of the Committee on Resolutions, and/or a member of the Convention's special committees.

30. **Representation From Qualified States and Territories:**

    A. When the cooperating Baptist churches in a state or defined territory have fifteen thousand (15,000) members, an initial application may be filed for representation on the Executive Committee, the Committee on Committees, and the Committee on Nominations.

B. When the cooperating Baptist churches have twenty thousand (20,000) members, an updated application may be filed for representation on the International Mission Board, North American Mission Board, and LifeWay Christian Resources of the Southern Baptist Convention, unless otherwise provided in the Board's charter.

C. When the cooperating Baptist churches have twenty-five thousand (25,000) members, an updated application may be filed for representation on GuideStone Financial Resources, the commissions, and institutions, unless otherwise provided in the commission's or institution's charter, and on the standing committees of the Convention, all as provided by the Bylaws of the Convention.

D. The application in each instance shall be filed with the Executive Committee, through its president, prior to its February meeting. The application shall contain information as specified by the Executive Committee.

E. Upon receiving the initial application, the Executive Committee shall investigate all matters pertaining to the request and make a recommendation to the Southern Baptist Convention at its next annual meeting. If the recommendation of the Executive Committee is favorable to the application, a copy of the recommendation shall be forwarded to the president of the Southern Baptist Convention and the chairman of the Committee on Committees prior to the next annual meeting of the Convention.

F. Upon receipt of the favorable recommendation of the Executive Committee on the initial application in (1) above, the president of the Convention, in conference with the vice presidents, shall appoint two (2) persons from the state or territory to serve as members of the Committee on Committees, and the Committee on Committees shall nominate two (2) persons from the state or territory to serve on the Committee on Nominations, all conditional upon the approval of the application by the Southern Baptist Convention.

G. Those elected by the Convention shall be immediately eligible to begin their appropriate terms of service

31. **Adoption of Reports:** The adoption of recommendations contained in reports to the Convention shall not bind the Convention on any other matters in the body of the reports; but the Convention reserves the right to consider and amend the body of all reports.

32. **As to Violation of State Laws:** All incorporated entities of the Convention shall be required to comply with the letter and spirit of the Constitution insofar as it is not in conflict with the statute law of the state in which an entity is incorporated, and nothing herein contained shall be construed to require any such incorporated entity to act and carry on its affairs in conflict with the

law of the state of its incorporation. In case any action of any entity of the Convention is found to be a violation of the law of the state of its incorporation, said action shall be reported by that entity to the Convention for appropriate action.

33. **Charters of Entities, Subsidiaries, and Ancillary Organizations:** The charters of all entities of the Convention shall provide that the trustees or directors of such entities be elected by the Convention, and that the charters may not be further amended without the prior consent of the Convention. The charters of all subsidiaries of any entity of the Convention shall provide that they may not be further amended without the prior consent of the Convention or its Executive Committee. No entity of the Convention shall establish a subsidiary corporation or any other legal entity or form for conducting its affairs, nor acquire a controlling interest or greater than a 25 percent interest in any other corporation or business enterprise, until the Convention or its Executive Committee has approved the same and its governing instruments. An entity of the Convention shall not undertake through a subsidiary or by any other means any action which, if undertaken by the entity itself, would violate the Constitution, Bylaws, or Business and Financial Plan of the Convention.

34. **Quorum:** The quorum for conducting business during the annual meeting of the Southern Baptist Convention shall be a minimum of 25 percent of those duly registered and seated messengers.

35. **Trustee Absenteeism:**

   A. Upon the request of any entity, the Convention may remove from office any trustee/director of that entity who has excessive unexcused absences. Following such removal, the Convention shall elect a successor to complete the term of office of the person removed.

   B. An entity shall give written notice of any request to remove a trustee/director for absenteeism at least one hundred twenty (120) days prior to the meeting of the Convention which shall consider the removal. The notice shall be given to the president of the Convention, the president/chief executive officer of the Executive Committee, the chairman of the Committee on Nominations, and the individual trustee/director whose removal shall be considered.

   C. If required by state law, an entity shall incorporate this procedure in its charter or bylaws prior to requesting the Convention to remove any trustee.

36. **Amendments:** The Bylaws may be amended pursuant to Bylaw 21 by a two-thirds majority vote at any time except during the last session of the Convention. Bylaw 14, which lists the entities and auxiliary of the Convention, may be amended by a majority vote of two (2) successive annual meetings.

# Business and Financial Plan of the Southern Baptist Convention[74]

I.   **Convention Budget:** Each entity of the Convention shall submit to the Executive Committee for its review:
   A.   an itemized estimate of its receipts for the next fiscal year, and
   B.   an itemized estimate of its expenditures for the next fiscal year according to the rule set forth below (See Section II-C) for making operating budgets.

The Executive Committee shall present to the Convention a budget, which budget shall consist of all the budgets of all the entities which have been submitted to the Executive Committee and reviewed by it, and recommend the amount of Convention funds to be allocated to each cause or entity.

II.  **Operating Budgets:**
   A.   *Convention Operating Budget*—The Executive Committee shall recommend to the Convention an operating budget which shall include all expenses

of the Convention, committees, and other items included in the Convention Operating Budget. The Executive Committee shall also recommend to the Convention the source of these funds.

B. *Entities Not Sharing in Table of Percentages*—The entities of the Convention not sharing in the table of percentages for distribution of funds shall be provided for as follows:

1. Expenses of Standing Committees—The Executive Committee shall approve or recommend to the Convention, after a personal conference or correspondence with chairpersons of standing committees, a sum of money to be appropriated to each of them for the Convention year.

2. Expenses of Special Committees—

    a. The expenses incurred by special committees appointed by the Convention to perform duties connected with one or more entities of the Convention shall be borne by the entity or entities concerned on a basis pro rata to receipts unless the expenses are otherwise specifically provided.

    b. The expenses incurred by special committees which do not directly concern any of the entities of the Convention shall be paid out of the Convention Operating Budget. Unless the amount of expenses is fixed by the Convention, the Executive Committee must agree to the amount to be expended before such expenditure is incurred.

c.  Itemized accounts of expenses of members of such committees shall be required and approved by the chairperson before the same shall be paid.

III.  **Convention Year:** The financial affairs of the Convention and all its entities, except those of the theological seminaries and GuideStone Financial Resources, shall be operated on the fiscal year beginning October 1 and closing September 30. The seminaries owned and operated under the authority of the Convention shall use the fiscal year beginning August 1 and closing July 31. GuideStone Financial Resources shall use the fiscal year beginning January 1 and closing December 31.

IV.  **The Disbursing Entity:** By agreement, all sums collected in the states for the causes fostered by this Convention will be forwarded at least monthly by each state office to the Executive Committee of this Convention, which shall act as the disbursing agent of this Convention. The Executive Committee shall remit at least weekly to each of the entities of the Convention the funds, distributable and designated, belonging to each entity. The first distribution in each month shall be on the seventh day of the month, or the nearest working day thereafter. The Executive Committee shall make monthly reports of receipts by states, and of disbursements by entities, and shall forward each month copies of these reports to the executives of the entities of the Convention, to the state offices, and to the denominational papers.

V.  **Distribution of Cooperative Program Receipts:** In order that the financial plans and purposes of the Convention

103

may operate successfully, the Convention appeals to its constituents to give to the whole Cooperative Program and to recognize the wisdom and right of the Convention to distribute its receipts from the Cooperative Program, thus assuring an equitable distribution among the entities of the Convention.

VI.  **Fund Raising Activities:**

A.  *Approval of Financial Activities*—No entity of the Southern Baptist Convention shall conduct any type of fund raising activity without the advance approval of the Convention, or its Executive Committee. No advance approval shall be required for the two Convention approved special offerings: Lottie Moon Christmas Offering for International Missions and Annie Armstrong Easter Offering for North American Missions.

B.  *Reporting Fund Raising Activities*—Each Convention entity shall report annually to the Executive Committee of the Southern Baptist Convention on any type of fund raising activity conducted by the entity. The report shall include a summary of the activity, its title, financial goals, structure, cost, and the results of such fund raising during the past year. No report shall be required for the Lottie Moon Christmas Offering for International Missions and the Annie Armstrong Easter Offering for North American Missions.

C.  *Cooperative Program Promotion*—Each Convention entity shall report on its efforts during the year in promoting Cooperative Program missions giving.

D. *No Financial Appeals to Churches*—In no case shall any Convention entity approach a church for inclusion in its church budget or appeal for financial contributions.

VII.  **Designated Gifts:** The Convention binds itself and its entities faithfully to apply and use such gifts as designated by the donor.

VIII.  **Trust Funds:** Each entity of the Convention is hereby instructed and ordered to keep all trust funds and designated gifts (for they are trust funds) sacred to the trust and designation; that they be kept separate from all other funds of such entity; that they are not to be used even temporarily for any other purpose than the purpose specified; and that such funds shall not hereafter be invested in the securities of any denominational body or entity.

IX.  **Gift Annuity Agreements:** All entities of this Convention writing gift annuity agreements in the future, and the Executive Committee when writing gift annuity agreements on behalf of the Southern Baptist Convention, are encouraged to place the annuity portion of each gift annuity on deposit with the Southern Baptist Foundation or GuideStone Financial Resources of the Southern Baptist Convention and enter into a contractual agreement with the Southern Baptist Foundation or GuideStone Financial Resources to pay the annuity payments required under the gift annuity agreement. This provision shall not apply to gifts of property, real or personal, the income of which is to go to the donor without further or additional obligation on the part of the entity accepting the gift. The Southern Baptist Foundation and GuideStone Financial Resources of the Southern Baptist

Convention shall, when determining the amounts required to fund the annuity portion of any gift annuity agreement, use mortality, interest, and expense rates which are approved or recommended by any appropriate regulatory authority, if any, or which are based on sound actuarial statistics.

X. **Indebtedness/Liability:** An entity or institution shall not create any liability or indebtedness, except such as can and will be repaid out of its anticipated receipts for current operations within a period of three (3) years, without the consent of the Convention or the Executive Committee. In order to obtain such approval, the entity must file a statement showing the source of such anticipated receipts.

Such consent must be likewise obtained for a purchase of properties (directly or indirectly or through ownership of controlling stock in other corporations or otherwise) subject to liens or encumbrances which cannot be repaid out of its anticipated receipts for current operations within a period of three (3) years.

XI. **Capital Fund Allocations:** Capital funds are allocated for the purpose of obtaining, expanding, improving, or maintaining properties owned by entities of the Southern Baptist Convention and essential to implementing entity program assignments.

Capital funds are used in projects which add to the long-range assets of the entity.

In making allocations for capital funds, priority shall be given to those projects which make the greatest contribution to advancing the overall objectives of the Southern Baptist Convention in bringing men to God through Jesus Christ.

Capital funds projects shall cost more than $5,000 and have a projected life span of more than five (5) years.

Items such as office equipment, furniture replacement, or books shall not be acquired through the capital fund allocation process.

Repairs and maintenance of income-producing property shall be made from earned income. Major repairs to non income-producing property may be considered as being eligible for capital fund allocations.

XII. **Contingent Reserves:** Each entity of this Convention shall set up as soon as possible a reserve for contingencies to provide for deficits that may occur either through decreased receipts or through emergencies or both. The maximum amount of contingent reserve of any entity shall be determined by the entity, subject to the approval of the Convention. Entities shall state on the balance sheets of the annual audits the amounts in Contingent Reserve Funds.

XIII. **Financial Report:**

A. *Audit Reports*—The entities of the Convention and the Executive Committee shall close their books and accounts as of the close of business on September 30 of each year, or July 31 in the case of the seminaries, or December 31 in the case of GuideStone Financial Resources, and have them audited by an independent certified public accountant (the external auditor) in accordance with auditing standards generally accepted in the United States of America.

Each entity of the Convention shall forward a copy of its external auditor's audit report (or, if more than one, all such reports) to the Executive Committee, as soon as possible after the close of its fiscal year. Additionally, as a part of this annual submission process, each entity shall also submit a statement signed by its chief executive officer and the chief financial officer which affirms that the books and accounts are accurate and complete to the best of the officer's knowledge, and that the officer believes the corporation's internal controls are adequate.

Each entity and the Executive Committee shall appoint a committee of its own trustees to undertake and accomplish duties pertinent to audit reports. These committees shall be appointed, and the trustees serving on the committees shall operate, independent of influence by their corporation's management, and each such committee shall include at least one trustee who is competent by training and experience in fiscal matters. The duties these committees shall perform for their respective entities shall include:

 1) recommending the appointment of the external auditor,

 2) studying the external auditor's audit report upon its completion,

 3) maintaining the independence of the entity's financial auditors,

4) reviewing the entity's critical accounting policies and decisions and the adequacy of its internal control systems,

5) preserving the integrity of the financial reporting process implemented by management, and

6) assuring that the business procedures listed in Article XVII are followed.

As a part of each external auditor's audit report, the external auditor shall prepare for the entity's audit committee a separate letter on the auditing firm's letterhead (the "management letter") in which the external auditor makes any recommendations concerning the entity's financial and accounting policies, processes, internal controls, or other matters. If the external auditor has no recommendations, he should so state in the management letter to the entity's audit committee. The entity's administration shall forward a copy of the management letter along with any comments that the administration might deem desirable to the Executive Committee simultaneously with the external auditor's audit report, for review and response (if appropriate) by the Executive Committee. The process of submission and review of the external auditors' audit reports and management letters of the several entities by the Executive Committee shall be governed by the assigned responsibilities and limitations upon authority described in SBC Bylaw 18 E and its subparagraphs (6), (7), (9), and (12).

When securities are placed for holding with a trustee (i.e. bank, trust company, foundation, etc.), a certified statement from such trustee should be made to the external auditor and be made a part of the annual external auditor's audit report or submitted as a supplement to the report.

B. *Printing of Reports*—The financial report of each entity and of the Executive Committee shall be printed in the Convention *Book of Reports*, or the Convention *Annual*, and shall contain the following six items, the first five of which come from its latest annual audit report:

1. Statement of Financial Position
2. Statement of Activities (revenues, expenses, and other changes in net assets)
3. Statement of Cash Flows
4. Classified list of investments by fund and type of investment
5. Receipts by states of contributions. These should show:
   a. Cooperative Program receipts received through the Executive Committee
   b. Designated receipts received through the Executive Committee
   c. Gifts not received through the Executive Committee
6. A statement executed by the chair of the entity's board attesting that the board's officers confirm the following fiscal conditions exist:

a. The expenses and perquisites of the president are not excessive and are in keeping with biblical stewardship, including every emolument and personal benefit of any kind (and specifically including housing, travel, automobile(s), and personal assistants) all valued at market rates.

b. All corporate expenses are reasonable and incurred to accomplish the entity's Organization Manual mission statement, Organization Manual ministry assignments, and any other responsibilities previously approved by the messengers of the Southern Baptist Convention and still in force.

c. All corporate expenses are incurred by the administration in a manner that reflects integrity and avoids appearances of impropriety while upholding a positive Christian witness to the Convention and beyond.

LifeWay Christian Resources shall include in its annual report to the Convention information on the amount of funds transferred to state conventions during the preceding year.

At the end of the presentation of entity financial data in each SBC *Book of Reports*, a statement shall be inserted which discloses that the entities have all supplied (or naming which have and which have not, if some have not) the statement required by Article XIII

111

B 6, above, and setting forth the elements thereof, in order that the messengers and the Convention's affiliated churches may be annually reassured that those fiscal conditions set forth are continuing to be maintained by the Convention's entities.

XIV. **Safeguarding of Funds:** All persons who transfer or safeguard funds or securities of the Convention or any entity of the Convention shall be bonded in an amount sufficient to protect against loss of the funds or securities involved. Such bonds may be reviewed and approved by the Convention or its Executive Committee.

Members of cooperating Southern Baptist churches shall have access to information from the records of Southern Baptist Convention entities regarding income, expenditures, debts, reserves, operating balances, and salary structures.

The securities of all Convention entities shall be held and maintained in a prudent manner, including under such internal controls as may be recommended in the entity's annual audit.

XV. **New Enterprises:** No new enterprise involving expenditure of money shall be authorized by the Convention except upon favorable action by the Convention in two (2) succeeding annual meetings; provided, however, that this restriction shall not apply to a recommendation of any entity of the Convention concerning its own work. In the event any new hospital propositions are made, they must be considered as new enterprises of the Convention, whether money is involved at the time of the acquiring of such property or not, and must be presented to two (2) succeeding annual sessions of the Convention.

XVI. **Appropriations by the Entities:** No entity shall make any appropriation to any cause or for any purpose other than for the promotion of its own work except by the approval or upon the instruction of the Convention or of the Executive Committee.

LifeWay Christian Resources shall be required to transfer funds to the Southern Baptist Convention each year to be used as the Convention determines. LifeWay Christian Resources shall not be permitted or required to transfer funds to other Southern Baptist Convention entities or committees.

XVII. **Business Procedure:** Entity boards of trustees should oversee the operations of the entity in such a manner as will assure effective and ethical management. Disclosures of the entity's relationship with other entities, its activities, liabilities, commitments, and results of operations should be accurate and complete and include all material information. The entity should not make any loan from funds of the entity to a trustee. The entity should not make any loan from funds of the entity to an officer or employee without having first obtained the approval of its board (or its delegated subcommittee) after disclosure of all relevant details. Employees and trustees should not appropriate for personal advantage any corporate property or business opportunities which should be enjoyed by the entity.

As a normal operating policy, each entity of the Southern Baptist Convention shall refrain from entering any business transaction with a trustee or employee, or a business enterprise in which a trustee or employee has an interest. An exception to this policy may be made, at the discretion of the board of trustees, in any case wherein it appears that a commodity or service is unavailable on a more favorable basis from any other source, or a commodity or service, at the discretion of the board, is found to be in the best interest of the entity. Competitive bids should be taken if possible. In any case being considered for exception, the extent of the trustee's or employee's interest shall be disclosed to the entire board.

XVIII. **Professional Services:** The Executive Committee at its discretion may employ an auditor to study the audited report with the auditors of the entities in the light of Convention instructions. The Executive Committee at its discretion may employ an engineer or architect to study proposed capital projects or maintenance of present capital assets.

XIX. **Publication and Merchandising Policy:** All entities of the Convention should give priority to using the services of LifeWay Christian Resources for editing, publishing, and distributing published materials that are to be sold. Entities may publish their own materials in print or digital form promoting their assigned ministries.

No entity other than LifeWay Christian Resources should be authorized to operate physical book stores at any location other than its principal office.

The Executive Committee of the Southern Baptist Convention may review the financial agreements entered into by LifeWay Christian Resources and other Convention entities and should, whenever appropriate, recommend changes in Convention policies and revisions of existing policies related to such agreements. At the request of any Convention entity, this committee should also suggest to LifeWay Christian Resources and other Convention entities steps they should take to resolve any disagreements that arise concerning financial agreements.

No entity shall publish a printed or digital format periodical, for general distribution to the churches or to members of the churches, if the Convention or its Executive Committee votes to request the periodical not be published.

XX. **Publications:** The plans and methods herein set forth shall be published each year in the Convention *Annual*, following the Bylaws of the Convention.

XXI. **Amendments:** This Business and Financial Plan may be amended by two-thirds of the messengers present and voting at any time except during the last session of the Convention.

# Baptist Faith and Message[75]

## (adopted June 14, 2000)

## I. The Scriptures

The Holy Bible was written by men divinely inspired and is God's revelation of Himself to man. It is a perfect treasure of divine instruction. It has God for its author, salvation for its end, and truth, without any mixture of error, for its matter. Therefore, all Scripture is totally true and trustworthy. It reveals the principles by which God judges us, and therefore is, and will remain to the end of the world, the true center of Christian union, and the supreme standard by which all human conduct, creeds, and religious opinions should be tried. All Scripture is a testimony to Christ, who is Himself the focus of divine revelation.

*Exodus 24: 4; Deuteronomy 4: 1–2; 17: 19; Joshua 8: 34; Psalms 19: 7–10; 119: 11, 89, 105, 140; Isaiah 34: 16; 40: 8; Jeremiah 15: 16; 36: 1–32; Matthew 5: 17–18; 22: 29; Luke 21: 33; 24: 44–46; John 5: 39; 16: 13–15; 17: 17; Acts 2: 16ff.; 17: 11; Romans 15: 4;*

16: 25–26; 2 Timothy 3: 15–17; Hebrews 1: 1–2; 4: 12; 1 Peter 1: 25; 2 Peter 1: 19–21.

# II. God

There is one and only one living and true God. He is an intelligent, spiritual, and personal Being, the Creator, Redeemer, Preserver, and Ruler of the universe. God is infinite in holiness and all other perfections. God is all powerful and all knowing; and His perfect knowledge extends to all things, past, present, and future, including the future decisions of His free creatures. To Him we owe the highest love, reverence, and obedience. The eternal triune God reveals Himself to us as Father, Son, and Holy Spirit, with distinct personal attributes, but without division of nature, essence, or being.

## A. God the Father

God as Father reigns with providential care over His universe, His creatures, and the flow of the stream of human history according to the purposes of His grace. He is all powerful, all knowing, all loving, and all wise. God is Father in truth to those who become children of God through faith in Jesus Christ. He is fatherly in His attitude toward all men.

*Genesis 1: 1; 2: 7; Exodus 3: 14; 6: 2–3; 15: 11ff.; 20; Leviticus 22: 2; Deuteronomy 6: 4; 32: 6; 1 Chronicles 29: 10; Psalm 19: 1–3; Isaiah 43: 3, 15; 64: 8; Jeremiah 10: 10; 17: 13; Matthew 6: 9ff.; 7: 11; 23: 9; 28: 19; Mark 1: 9–11; John 4: 24; 5: 26; 14: 6–13; 17: 1–8; Acts 1: 7; Romans 8: 14–15; 1 Corinthians 8: 6; Galatians*

*4: 6; Ephesians 4: 6; Colossians 1: 15; 1 Timothy 1: 17; Hebrews*
*11: 6; 12: 9; 1 Peter 1: 17; 1 John 5: 7.*

## B. God the Son

Christ is the eternal Son of God. In His incarnation as Jesus
Christ He was conceived of the Holy Spirit and born of the vir-
gin Mary. Jesus perfectly revealed and did the will of God, taking upon Himself human nature with its demands and necessities
and identifying Himself completely with mankind yet without
sin. He honored the divine law by His personal obedience, and
in His substitutionary death on the cross He made provision for
the redemption of men from sin. He was raised from the dead
with a glorified body and appeared to His disciples as the person who was with them before His crucifixion. He ascended
into heaven and is now exalted at the right hand of God where
He is the One Mediator, fully God, fully man, in whose Person
is effected the reconciliation between God and man. He will
return in power and glory to judge the world and to consummate
His redemptive mission. He now dwells in all believers as the
living and ever present Lord.

*Genesis 18; Psalms 2: 7ff.; 110; Isaiah 7: 14; 53: 1–12; Matthew*
*1: 18–23; 3: 17; 8: 29; 11: 27; 14: 33; 16: 16, 27; 17: 5; 27; 28: 1–6,*
*19; Mark 1: 1; 3: 11; Luke 1: 35; 4: 41; 22: 70; 24: 46; John 1: 1–18,*
*29; 10: 30, 38; 11: 25–27; 12: 44–50; 14: 7–11; 16: 15–16, 28;*
*17: 1–5, 21–22; 20: 1–20, 28; Acts 1: 9; 2: 22–24; 7: 55–56;*
*9: 4–5, 20; Romans 1: 3–4; 3: 23–26; 5: 6–21; 8: 1–3, 34; 10: 4;*
*1 Corinthians 1: 30; 2: 2; 8: 6; 15: 1–8, 24–28; 2 Corinthians*
*5: 19–21; 8: 9; Galatians 4: 4–5; Ephesians 1: 20; 3: 11; 4: 7–10;*

*Philippians 2: 5–11; Colossians 1: 13–22; 2: 9; 1 Thessalonians 4: 14–18; 1 Timothy 2: 5–6; 3: 16; Titus 2: 13–14; Hebrews 1: 1–3; 4: 14–15; 7: 14–28; 9: 12–15, 24–28; 12: 2; 13: 8; 1 Peter 2: 21–25; 3: 22; 1 John 1: 7–9; 3: 2; 4: 14–15; 5: 9; 2 John 7–9; Revelation 1: 13–16; 5: 9–14; 12: 10–11; 13: 8; 19: 16.*

## C. God the Holy Spirit

The Holy Spirit is the Spirit of God, fully divine. He inspired holy men of old to write the Scriptures. Through illumination He enables men to understand truth. He exalts Christ. He convicts men of sin, of righteousness, and of judgment. He calls men to the Savior, and effects regeneration. At the moment of regeneration He baptizes every believer into the Body of Christ. He cultivates Christian character, comforts believers, and bestows the spiritual gifts by which they serve God through His church. He seals the believer unto the day of final redemption. His presence in the Christian is the guarantee that God will bring the believer into the fullness of the stature of Christ. He enlightens and empowers the believer and the church in worship, evangelism, and service.

*Genesis 1: 2; Judges 14: 6; Job 26: 13; Psalms 51: 11; 139: 7ff.; Isaiah 61: 1–3; Joel 2: 28–32; Matthew 1: 18; 3: 16; 4: 1; 12: 28–32; 28: 19; Mark 1: 10, 12; Luke 1: 35; 4: 1, 18–19; 11: 13; 12: 12; 24: 49; John 4: 24; 14: 16–17, 26; 15: 26; 16: 7–14; Acts 1: 8; 2: 1–4, 38; 4: 31; 5: 3; 6: 3; 7: 55; 8: 17, 39; 10: 44; 13: 2; 15: 28; 16: 6; 19: 1–6; Romans 8: 9–11, 14–16, 26–27; 1 Corinthians 2: 10–14; 3: 16; 12: 3–11, 13; Galatians 4: 6; Ephesians 1: 13–14; 4: 30; 5: 18; 1 Thessalonians 5: 19; 1 Timothy 3: 16; 4: 1; 2 Timothy*

*1: 14; 3: 16; Hebrews 9: 8, 14; 2 Peter 1: 21; 1 John 4: 13; 5: 6–7;*
*Revelation 1: 10; 22: 17.*

# III. Man

Man is the special creation of God, made in His own image.
He created them male and female as the crowning work of
His creation. The gift of gender is thus part of the goodness
of God's creation. In the beginning man was innocent of sin
and was endowed by his Creator with freedom of choice. By
his free choice man sinned against God and brought sin into
the human race. Through the temptation of Satan man trans-
gressed the command of God, and fell from his original inno-
cence whereby his posterity inherit a nature and an environment
inclined toward sin. Therefore, as soon as they are capable of
moral action, they become transgressors and are under condem-
nation. Only the grace of God can bring man into His holy fellowship and enable man to fulfill the creative purpose of God.
The sacredness of human personality is evident in that God created man in His own image, and in that Christ died for man;
therefore, every person of every race possesses full dignity and is
worthy of respect and Christian love.

*Genesis 1: 26–30; 2: 5, 7, 18–22; 3; 9: 6; Psalms 1; 8: 3–6; 32: 1–5;*
*51: 5; Isaiah 6: 5; Jeremiah 17: 5; Matthew 16: 26; Acts 17: 26–31;*
*Romans 1: 19–32; 3: 10–18, 23; 5: 6, 12, 19; 6: 6; 7: 14–25;*
*8: 14–18, 29; 1 Corinthians 1: 21–31; 15: 19, 21–22; Ephesians*
*2: 1–22; Colossians 1: 21–22; 3: 9–11.*

# IV. Salvation

Salvation involves the redemption of the whole man, and is offered freely to all who accept Jesus Christ as Lord and Savior, who by His own blood obtained eternal redemption for the believer. In its broadest sense salvation includes regeneration, justification, sanctification, and glorification. There is no salvation apart from personal faith in Jesus Christ as Lord.

A. Regeneration, or the new birth, is a work of God's grace whereby believers become new creatures in Christ Jesus. It is a change of heart wrought by the Holy Spirit through conviction of sin, to which the sinner responds in repentance toward God and faith in the Lord Jesus Christ. Repentance and faith are inseparable experiences of grace.

Repentance is a genuine turning from sin toward God. Faith is the acceptance of Jesus Christ and commitment of the entire personality to Him as Lord and Savior.

B. Justification is God's gracious and full acquittal upon principles of His righteousness of all sinners who repent and believe in Christ. Justification brings the believer unto a relationship of peace and favor with God.

C. Sanctification is the experience, beginning in regeneration, by which the believer is set apart to God's purposes, and is enabled to progress toward moral and spiritual maturity through the presence and power of the Holy Spirit dwelling in him. Growth in grace should continue throughout the regenerate person's life.

D. Glorification is the culmination of salvation and is the final blessed and abiding state of the redeemed.

*Genesis 3: 15; Exodus 3: 14–17; 6: 2–8; Matthew 1: 21; 4: 17; 16: 21–26; 27: 22–28: 6; Luke 1: 68–69; 2: 28–32; John 1: 11–14, 29; 3: 3–21, 36; 5: 24; 10: 9, 28–29; 15: 1–16; 17: 17; Acts 2: 21; 4: 12; 15: 11; 16: 30–31; 17: 30–31; 20: 32; Romans 1: 16–18; 2: 4; 3: 23–25; 4: 3ff.; 5: 8–10; 6: 1–23; 8: 1–18, 29–39; 10: 9–10, 13; 13: 11–14; 1 Corinthians 1: 18, 30; 6: 19–20; 15: 10; 2 Corinthians 5: 17–20; Galatians 2: 20; 3: 13; 5: 22–25; 6: 15; Ephesians 1: 7; 2: 8–22; 4: 11–16; Philippians 2: 12–13; Colossians 1: 9–22; 3; 1 Thessalonians 5: 23–24; 2 Timothy 1: 12; Titus 2: 11–14; Hebrews 2: 1–3; 5: 8–9; 9: 24–28; 11: 1–12: 8, 14; James 2: 14–26; 1 Peter 1: 2–23; 1 John 1: 6–2: 11; Revelation 3: 20; 21: 1–22: 5.*

# V. God's Purpose of Grace

Election is the gracious purpose of God, according to which He regenerates, justifies, sanctifies, and glorifies sinners. It is consistent with the free agency of man, and comprehends all the means in connection with the end. It is the glorious display of God's sovereign goodness, and is infinitely wise, holy, and unchangeable. It excludes boasting and promotes humility.

All true believers endure to the end. Those whom God has accepted in Christ, and sanctified by His Spirit, will never fall away from the state of grace, but shall persevere to the end. Believers may fall into sin through neglect and temptation, whereby they grieve the Spirit, impair their graces and comforts, and bring reproach on the cause of Christ and temporal judgments on themselves; yet they shall be kept by the power of God through faith unto salvation.

*Genesis 12: 1–3; Exodus 19: 5–8; 1 Samuel 8: 4–7, 19–22; Isaiah 5: 1–7; Jeremiah 31: 31ff.; Matthew 16: 18–19; 21: 28–45; 24: 22, 31; 25: 34; Luke 1: 68–79; 2: 29–32; 19: 41–44; 24: 44–48; John 1: 12–14; 3: 16; 5: 24; 6: 44–45, 65; 10: 27–29; 15: 16; 17: 6, 12, 17–18; Acts 20: 32; Romans 5: 9–10; 8: 28–39; 10: 12–15; 11: 5–7, 26–36; 1 Corinthians 1: 1–2; 15: 24–28; Ephesians 1: 4–23; 2: 1–10; 3: 1–11; Colossians 1: 12–14; 2 Thessalonians 2: 13–14; 2 Timothy 1: 12; 2: 10, 19; Hebrews 11: 39–12: 2; James 1: 12; 1 Peter 1: 2–5, 13; 2: 4–10; 1 John 1: 7–9; 2: 19; 3: 2.*

# VI. The Church

A New Testament church of the Lord Jesus Christ is an autonomous local congregation of baptized believers, associated by covenant in the faith and fellowship of the Gospel; observing the two ordinances of Christ, governed by His laws, exercising the gifts, rights, and privileges invested in them by His Word, and seeking to extend the Gospel to the ends of the earth. Each congregation operates under the Lordship of Christ through democratic processes. In such a congregation each member is responsible and accountable to Christ as Lord. Its scriptural officers are pastors and deacons. While both men and women are gifted for service in the church, the office of pastor is limited to men as qualified by Scripture.

The New Testament speaks also of the church as the Body of Christ which includes all of the redeemed of all the ages, believers from every tribe, and tongue, and people, and nation.

*Matthew 16: 15–19; 18: 15–20; Acts 2: 41–42, 47; 5: 11–14; 6: 3–6; 13: 1–3; 14: 23, 27; 15: 1–30; 16: 5; 20: 28; Romans 1: 7;*

*1 Corinthians 1: 2; 3: 16; 5: 4–5; 7: 17; 9: 13–14; 12; Ephesians 1: 22–23; 2: 19–22; 3: 8–11, 21; 5: 22–32; Philippians 1: 1; Colossians 1: 18; 1 Timothy 2: 9–14; 3: 1–15; 4: 14; Hebrews 11: 39–40; 1 Peter 5: 1–4; Revelation 2–3; 21: 2–3.*

# VII. Baptism and the Lord's Supper

Christian baptism is the immersion of a believer in water in the name of the Father, the Son, and the Holy Spirit. It is an act of obedience symbolizing the believer's faith in a crucified, buried, and risen Savior, the believer's death to sin, the burial of the old life, and the resurrection to walk in newness of life in Christ Jesus. It is a testimony to his faith in the final resurrection of the dead. Being a church ordinance, it is prerequisite to the privileges of church membership and to the Lord's Supper.

The Lord's Supper is a symbolic act of obedience whereby members of the church, through partaking of the bread and the fruit of the vine, memorialize the death of the Redeemer and anticipate His second coming.

*Matthew 3: 13–17; 26: 26–30; 28: 19–20; Mark 1: 9–11; 14: 22–26; Luke 3: 21–22; 22: 19–20; John 3: 23; Acts 2: 41–42; 8: 35–39; 16: 30–33; 20: 7; Romans 6: 3–5; 1 Corinthians 10: 16, 21; 11: 23–29; Colossians 2: 12.*

# VIII. The Lord's Day

The first day of the week is the Lord's Day. It is a Christian institution for regular observance. It commemorates the resurrection of Christ from the dead and should include exercises of worship and spiritual devotion, both public and private. Activities on the Lord's Day should be commensurate with the Christian's conscience under the Lordship of Jesus Christ.

*Exodus 20: 8–11; Matthew 12: 1–12; 28; Mark 2: 27–28; 16: 1–7; Luke 24: 1–3, 33–36; John 4: 21–24; 20: 1, 19–28; Acts 20: 7; Romans 14: 5–10; 1 Corinthians 16: 1–2; Colossians 2: 16; 3: 16; Revelation 1: 10.*

# IX. The Kingdom

The Kingdom of God includes both His general sovereignty over the universe and His particular kingship over men who willfully acknowledge Him as King. Particularly the Kingdom is the realm of salvation into which men enter by trustful, childlike commitment to Jesus Christ. Christians ought to pray and to labor that the Kingdom may come and God's will be done on earth. The full consummation of the Kingdom awaits the return of Jesus Christ and the end of this age.

*Genesis 1: 1; Isaiah 9: 6–7; Jeremiah 23: 5–6; Matthew 3: 2; 4: 8–10, 23; 12: 25–28; 13: 1–52; 25: 31–46; 26: 29; Mark 1: 14–15; 9: 1; Luke 4: 43; 8: 1; 9: 2; 12: 31–32; 17: 20–21; 23: 42; John 3: 3; 18: 36; Acts 1: 6–7; 17: 22–31; Romans 5: 17; 8: 19; 1 Corinthians 15: 24–28; Colossians 1: 13; Hebrews 11: 10, 16; 12: 28; 1 Peter 2: 4–10; 4: 13; Revelation 1: 6, 9; 5: 10; 11: 15; 21–22.*

# X. Last Things

God, in His own time and in His own way, will bring the world to its appropriate end. According to His promise, Jesus Christ will return personally and visibly in glory to the earth; the dead will be raised; and Christ will judge all men in righteousness. The unrighteous will be consigned to Hell, the place of everlasting punishment. The righteous in their resurrected and glorified bodies will receive their reward and will dwell forever in Heaven with the Lord.

*Isaiah 2: 4; 11: 9; Matthew 16: 27; 18: 8–9; 19: 28; 24: 27, 30, 36, 44; 25: 31–46; 26: 64; Mark 8: 38; 9: 43–48; Luke 12: 40, 48; 16: 19–26; 17: 22–37; 21: 27–28; John 14: 1–3; Acts 1: 11; 17: 31; Romans 14: 10; 1 Corinthians 4: 5; 15: 24–28, 35–58; 2 Corinthians 5: 10; Philippians 3: 20–21; Colossians 1: 5; 3: 4; 1 Thessalonians 4: 14–18; 5; 2 Thessalonians 1: 7ff.; 2; 1 Timothy 6: 14; 2 Timothy 4: 1, 8; Titus 2: 13; Hebrews 9: 27–28; James 5: 8; 2 Peter 3: 7ff.; 1 John 2: 28; 3: 2; Jude 14; Revelation 1: 18; 3: 11; 20: 1–22: 13.*

# XI. Evangelism and Missions

It is the duty and privilege of every follower of Christ and of every church of the Lord Jesus Christ to endeavor to make disciples of all nations. The new birth of man's spirit by God's Holy Spirit means the birth of love for others. Missionary effort on the part of all rests thus upon a spiritual necessity of the regenerate life, and is expressly and repeatedly commanded in the teachings of Christ. The Lord Jesus Christ has commanded the preaching of the Gospel to all nations. It is the duty of every child of God to seek constantly to win the lost to Christ by verbal witness undergirded by a Christian lifestyle, and by other methods in harmony with the Gospel of Christ.

*Genesis 12: 1–3; Exodus 19: 5–6; Isaiah 6: 1–8; Matthew 9: 37–38; 10: 5–15; 13: 18–30, 37–43; 16: 19; 22: 9–10; 24: 14; 28: 18–20; Luke 10: 1–18; 24: 46–53; John 14: 11–12; 15: 7–8, 16; 17: 15; 20: 21; Acts 1: 8; 2; 8: 26–40; 10: 42–48; 13: 2–3; Romans 10: 13–15; Ephesians 3: 1–11; 1 Thessalonians 1: 8; 2 Timothy 4: 5; Hebrews 2: 1–3; 11: 39–12: 2; 1 Peter 2: 4–10; Revelation 22: 17.*

# XII. Education

Christianity is the faith of enlightenment and intelligence. In Jesus Christ abide all the treasures of wisdom and knowledge. All sound learning is, therefore, a part of our Christian heritage. The new birth opens all human faculties and creates a thirst for knowledge. Moreover, the cause of education in the Kingdom of Christ is co-ordinate with the causes of missions and general benevolence, and should receive along with these the liberal support of the churches. An adequate system of Christian education is necessary to a complete spiritual program for Christ's people.

In Christian education there should be a proper balance between academic freedom and academic responsibility. Freedom in any orderly relationship of human life is always limited and never absolute. The freedom of a teacher in a Christian school, college, or seminary is limited by the pre-eminence of Jesus Christ, by the authoritative nature of the Scriptures, and by the distinct purpose for which the school exists.

*Deuteronomy 4: 1, 5, 9, 14; 6: 1–10; 31: 12–13; Nehemiah 8: 1–8; Job 28: 28; Psalms 19: 7ff.; 119: 11; Proverbs 3: 13ff.; 4: 1–10; 8: 1–7, 11; 15: 14; Ecclesiastes 7: 19; Matthew 5: 2; 7: 24ff.; 28: 19–20; Luke 2: 40; 1 Corinthians 1: 18–31; Ephesians 4: 11–16; Philippians 4: 8;*

*Colossians 2: 3, 8–9; 1 Timothy 1: 3–7; 2 Timothy 2: 15; 3: 14–17; Hebrews 5: 12–6: 3; James 1: 5; 3: 17.*

# XIII. Stewardship

God is the source of all blessings, temporal and spiritual; all that we have and are we owe to Him. Christians have a spiritual debtorship to the whole world, a holy trusteeship in the Gospel, and a binding stewardship in their possessions. They are therefore under obligation to serve Him with their time, talents, and material possessions; and should recognize all these as entrusted to them to use for the glory of God and for helping others. According to the Scriptures, Christians should contribute of their means cheerfully, regularly, systematically, proportionately, and liberally for the advancement of the Redeemer's cause on earth.

*Genesis 14: 20; Leviticus 27: 30–32; Deuteronomy 8: 18; Malachi 3: 8–12; Matthew 6: 1–4,19–21; 19: 21; 23: 23; 25: 14–29; Luke 12: 16–21, 42; 16: 1–13; Acts 2: 44–47; 5: 1–11; 17: 24–25; 20: 35; Romans 6: 6–22; 12: 1–2; 1 Corinthians 4: 1–2; 6: 19–20; 12; 16: 1–4; 2 Corinthians 8–9; 12: 15; Philippians 4: 10–19; 1 Peter 1: 18–19.*

# XIV. Cooperation

Christ's people should, as occasion requires, organize such associations and conventions as may best secure cooperation for the great objects of the Kingdom of God. Such organizations have no authority over one another or over the churches. They are voluntary and advisory bodies designed to elicit, combine, and direct the energies of our people in the most effective manner. Members of New Testament churches should cooperate with one another in carrying forward the missionary, educational, and benevolent ministries for the extension of Christ's Kingdom. Christian unity in the New Testament sense is spiritual harmony and voluntary cooperation for common ends by various groups of Christ's people. Cooperation is desirable between the various Christian denominations, when the end to be attained is itself justified, and when such cooperation involves no violation of conscience or compromise of loyalty to Christ and His Word as revealed in the New Testament.

*Exodus 17: 12; 18: 17ff.; Judges 7: 21; Ezra 1: 3–4; 2: 68–69; 5: 14–15; Nehemiah 4; 8: 1–5; Matthew 10: 5–15; 20: 1–16; 22: 1–10; 28: 19–20; Mark 2: 3; Luke 10; Acts 1: 13–14; 2; 4: 31–37; 13: 2–3; 15: 1–35; 1 Corinthians 1: 10–17; 3: 5–15; 12; 2 Corinthians 8–9; Galatians 1: 6–10; Ephesians 4: 1–16; Philippians 1: 15–18.*

# XV. The Christian and the Social Order

All Christians are under obligation to seek to make the will of Christ supreme in our own lives and in human society. Means and methods used for the improvement of society and the establishment of righteousness among men can be truly and permanently helpful only when they are rooted in the regeneration of the individual by the saving grace of God in Jesus Christ. In the spirit of Christ, Christians should oppose racism, every form of greed, selfishness, and vice, and all forms of sexual immorality, including adultery, homosexuality, and pornography. We should work to provide for the orphaned, the needy, the abused, the aged, the helpless, and the sick. We should speak on behalf of the unborn and contend for the sanctity of all human life from conception to natural death. Every Christian should seek to bring industry, government, and society as a whole under the sway of the principles of righteousness, truth, and brotherly love. In order to promote these ends Christians should be ready to work with all men of good will in any good cause, always being careful to act in the spirit of love without compromising their loyalty to Christ and His truth.

*Exodus 20: 3–17; Leviticus 6: 2–5; Deuteronomy 10: 12; 27: 17; Psalm 101: 5; Micah 6: 8; Zechariah 8: 16; Matthew 5: 13–16, 43–48; 22: 36–40; 25: 35; Mark 1: 29–34; 2: 3ff.; 10: 21; Luke 4: 18–21; 10: 27–37; 20: 25; John 15: 12; 17: 15; Romans 12–14; 1 Corinthians 5: 9–10; 6: 1–7; 7: 20–24; 10: 23–11: 1; Galatians 3: 26–28; Ephesians 6: 5–9; Colossians 3: 12–17; 1 Thessalonians 3: 12; Philemon; James 1: 27; 2: 8.*

# XVI. Peace and War

It is the duty of Christians to seek peace with all men on principles of righteousness. In accordance with the spirit and teachings of Christ they should do all in their power to put an end to war.

The true remedy for the war spirit is the Gospel of our Lord. The supreme need of the world is the acceptance of His teachings in all the affairs of men and nations, and the practical application of His law of love. Christian people throughout the world should pray for the reign of the Prince of Peace.

*Isaiah 2: 4; Matthew 5: 9, 38–48; 6: 33; 26: 52; Luke 22: 36, 38;*
*Romans 12: 18–19; 13: 1–7; 14: 19; Hebrews 12: 14; James 4: 1–2.*

# XVII. Religious Liberty

God alone is Lord of the conscience, and He has left it free
from the doctrines and commandments of men which are contrary to His Word or not contained in it. Church and state
should be separate. The state owes to every church protection
and full freedom in the pursuit of its spiritual ends. In providing for such freedom no ecclesiastical group or denomination
should be favored by the state more than others. Civil government being ordained of God, it is the duty of Christians to
render loyal obedience thereto in all things not contrary to the
revealed will of God. The church should not resort to the civil
power to carry on its work. The Gospel of Christ contemplates
spiritual means alone for the pursuit of its ends. The state has
no right to impose penalties for religious opinions of any kind.
The state has no right to impose taxes for the support of any
form of religion. A free church in a free state is the Christian
ideal, and this implies the right of free and unhindered access
to God on the part of all men, and the right to form and propa-
gate opinions in the sphere of religion without interference by
the civil power.

*Genesis 1: 27; 2: 7; Matthew 6: 6–7, 24; 16: 26; 22: 21; John*
*8: 36; Acts 4: 19–20; Romans 6: 1–2; 13: 1–7; Galatians 5: 1, 13;*
*Philippians 3: 20; 1 Timothy 2: 1–2; James 4: 12; 1 Peter 2: 12–17;*
*3: 11–17; 4: 12–19.*

# XVIII. The Family

God has ordained the family as the foundational institution of human society. It is composed of persons related to one another by marriage, blood, or adoption.

Marriage is the uniting of one man and one woman in covenant commitment for a lifetime. It is God's unique gift to reveal the union between Christ and His church and to provide for the man and the woman in marriage the framework for intimate companionship, the channel of sexual expression according to biblical standards, and the means for procreation of the human race.

The husband and wife are of equal worth before God, since both are created in God's image. The marriage relationship models the way God relates to His people. A husband is to love his wife as Christ loved the church. He has the God-given responsibility to provide for, to protect, and to lead his family. A wife is to submit herself graciously to the servant leadership of her husband even as the church willingly submits to the headship of Christ. She, being in the image of God as is her husband and thus equal to him, has the God-given responsibility to respect her husband and to serve as his helper in managing the household and nurturing the next generation.

Children, from the moment of conception, are a blessing and heritage from the Lord. Parents are to demonstrate to their children God's pattern for marriage. Parents are to teach their children spiritual and moral values and to lead them, through consistent lifestyle example and loving discipline, to make choices based on biblical truth. Children are to honor and obey their parents.

*Genesis 1: 26–28; 2: 15–25; 3: 1–20; Exodus 20: 12; Deuteronomy 6: 4–9; Joshua 24: 15; 1 Samuel 1: 26–28; Psalms 51: 5; 78: 1–8; 127; 128; 139: 13–16; Proverbs 1: 8; 5: 15–20; 6: 20–22; 12: 4; 13: 24; 14: 1; 17: 6; 18: 22; 22: 6, 15; 23: 13–14; 24: 3; 29: 15, 17; 31: 10–31; Ecclesiastes 4: 9–12; 9: 9; Malachi 2: 14–16; Matthew 5: 31–32; 18: 2–5; 19: 3–9; Mark 10: 6–12; Romans 1: 18–32; 1 Corinthians 7: 1–16; Ephesians 5: 21–33; 6: 1–4; Colossians 3: 18–21; 1 Timothy 5: 8, 14; 2 Timothy 1: 3–5; Titus 2: 3–5; Hebrews 13: 4; 1 Peter 3: 1–7.*

# Appendix A

# Southern Baptist Convention Presidents

| Years Elected | President |
|---|---|
| 1845,[1] 1846,[2] 1849[3] | William Bullein Johnson |
| 1851,[4] 1853,[5] 1855,[6] 1857[7] | R.B.C. Howell |
| 1859,[8] 1861[9] | Richard Fuller |
| 1863,[10] 1866,[11] 1867,[12] 1868,[13] 1869,[14] 1870,[15] 1871[16] | Patrick Hues Mell |
| 1872,[17] 1873,[18] 1874,[19] 1875,[20] 1876,[21] 1877,[22] 1878,[23] 1879[24] | James Petrigru Boyce |
| 1880,[25] 1881,[26] 1882,[27] 1883,[28] 1884,[29] 1885,[30] 1886,[31] 1887[32] | Patrick Hues Mell |
| 1888[33] | James Petigru Boyce |
| 1889,[34] 1890,[35] 1891,[36] 1892,[37] 1893,[38] 1894,[39] 1895,[40] 1896,[41] 1897,[42] 1898[43] | Jonathan Haralson |
| 1899,[44] 1900,[45] 1901[46] | William Jonathan Northen |
| 1902,[47] 1903,[48] 1904[49] | James Philip Eagle |
| 1905,[50] 1906,[51] 1907[52] | Edwin William Stephens |
| 1908,[53] 1909,[54] 1910[55] | Joshua Levering |
| 1911,[56] 1912,[57] 1913[58] | Edwin Charles Dargan |
| 1914,[59] 1915,[60] 1916[61] | Lansing Burrows |

| | |
|---|---|
| 1917,[62] 1918,[63] 1919,[64] 1920[65] | James Bruton Gambrell |
| 1921,[66] 1922,[67] 1923[68] | Edgar Young Mullins |
| 1924,[69] 1925,[70] 1926[71] | George White McDaniel |
| 1927,[72] 1928,[73] 1929[74] | George W. Truett |
| 1930,[75] 1931,[76] 1932[77] | William Joseph McGlothlin |
| 1932[78] | Fred F. Brown |
| 1933,[79] 1934[80] | M. E. Dodd |
| 1935,[81] 1936,[82] 1937[83] | John Richard Sampey |
| 1938,[84] 1939[85] | Lee Rutland Scarborough |
| 1940,[86] 1941[87] | William Wistar Hamilton |
| 1942,[88] 1944[89] | Pat M. Neff |
| 1946,[90] 1947[91] | Louie DeVotie Newton |
| 1948,[92] 1949,[93] 1950[94] | Robert Greene Lee |
| 1951,[95] 1952[96] | James David Grey |
| 1953,[97] 1954[98] | James Wilson Storer |
| 1955,[99] 1956[100] | Casper Carl Warren |
| 1957,[101] 1958[102] | Brooks Hays |
| 1959,[103] 1960[104] | Ramsey Pollard |
| 1961,[105] 1962[106] | Herschel Harold Hobbs |
| 1963[107] | Kenneth Owen White |
| 1964,[108] 1965[109] | William Wayne Dehoney |
| 1966,[110] 1967[111] | Henry Franklin Paschall |
| 1968,[112] 1969[113] | Wallie Amos Criswell |
| 1970,[114] 1971[115] | Carl E. Bates |
| 1972,[116] 1973[117] | Owen Cooper |
| 1974,[118] 1975[119] | Jaroy Weber |
| 1976[120] | James L. Sullivan |
| 1977,[121] 1978[122] | Jimmy Raymond Allen |
| 1979[123] | Adrian Rogers |
| 1980,[124] 1981[125] | Bailey E. Smith |
| 1982,[126] 1983[127] | James T. Draper Jr. |
| 1984,[128] 1985[129] | Charles F. Stanley |

| | |
|---|---|
| 1986,[130] 1987[131] | Adrian P. Rogers |
| 1988,[132] 1989[133] | C. Jerry Vines |
| 1990,[134] 1991[135] | Morris H. Chapman |
| 1992,[136] 1993[137] | H. Edwin Young |
| 1994,[138] 1995[139] | James B. Henry |
| 1996,[140] 1997[141] | Thomas D. Elliff |
| 1998,[142] 1999[143] | Paige Patterson |
| 2000,[144] 2001[145] | James Merritt |
| 2002,[146] 2003[147] | Jack Graham |
| 2004,[148] 2005[149] | Bobby Welch |
| 2006,[150] 2007[151] | Frank Page |
| 2008,[152] 2009[153] | Johnny Hunt |
| 2010,[154] 2011[155] | Bryant Wright |
| 2012,[156] 2013[157] | Fred Luter |
| 2014,[158] 2015[159] | Ronnie Floyd |
| 2016,[160] 2017[161] | Steve Gaines |

*William Bullein Johnson*

[1] 1845 SBC *Annual*, 12.
[2] 1846 SBC *Annual*, 3.
[3] 1849 SBC *Annual*, 32.
[4] 1851 SBC *Annual*, 5.
[5] 1853 SBC *Annual*, 5.
[6] 1855 SBC *Annual*, 3.
[7] 1857 SBC *Annual*, 5.
[8] 1859 SBC *Annual*, 13-14.
[9] 1861 SBC *Annual*, 9.
[10] 1863 SBC *Annual*, 11.
[11] 1866 SBC *Annual*, 12.
[12] 1867 SBC *Annual*, 12.
[13] 1868 SBC *Annual*, 12.
[14] 1869 SBC *Annual*, 11.
[15] 1870 SBC *Annual*, 13.
[16] 1871 SBC *Annual*, 13.
[17] 1872 SBC *Annual*, 12.
[18] 1873 SBC *Annual*, 12.
[19] 1874 SBC *Annual*, 12.
[20] 1875 SBC *Annual*, 12.
[21] 1876 SBC *Annual*, 9.
[22] 1877 SBC *Annual*, 9.
[23] 1878 SBC *Annual*, 10.
[24] 1879 SBC *Annual*, 13.
[25] 1880 SBC *Annual*, 11.
[26] 1881 SBC *Annual*, 9.
[27] 1882 SBC *Annual*, 12.
[28] 1883 SBC *Annual*, 12.
[29] 1884 SBC *Annual*, 12.
[30] 1885 SBC *Annual*, 11.
[31] 1886 SBC *Annual*, 11.
[32] 1887 SBC *Annual*, 13.
[33] 1888 SBC *Annual*, 7.
[34] 1889 SBC *Annual*, 8.
[35] 1890 SBC *Annual*, 7.
[36] 1891 SBC *Annual*, 7.

[37] 1892 SBC *Annual*, 9.
[38] 1893 SBC *Annual*, 9.
[39] 1894 SBC *Annual*, 9.
[40] 1895 SBC *Annual*, 11.
[41] 1896 SBC *Annual*, 12.
[42] 1897 SBC *Annual*, 11.
[43] 1898 SBC *Annual*, 13.
[44] 1899 SBC *Annual*, 13.
[45] 1900 SBC *Annual*, 9.
[46] 1901 SBC *Annual*, 9.
[47] 1902 SBC *Annual*, 10.
[48] 1903 SBC *Annual*, 9.
[49] 1904 SBC *Annual*, 1.
[50] 1905 SBC *Annual*, 1.
[51] 1906 SBC *Annual*, 2.
[52] 1907 SBC *Annual*, 9.
[53] 1908 SBC *Annual*, 1.
[54] 1909 SBC *Annual*, 1.
[55] 1910 SBC *Annual*, 1.
[56] 1911 SBC *Annual*, 2.
[57] 1912 SBC *Annual*, 10.
[58] 1913 SBC *Annual*, 12.
[59] 1914 SBC *Annual*, 12.
[60] 1915 SBC *Annual*, 14.
[61] 1916 SBC *Annual*, 15.
[62] 1917 SBC *Annual*, 17.
[63] 1918 SBC *Annual*, 13.
[64] 1919 SBC *Annual*, 15-16.
[65] 1920 SBC *Annual*, 22.
[66] 1921 SBC *Annual*, 21-22.
[67] 1922 SBC *Annual*, 16.
[68] 1923 SBC *Annual*, 18.
[69] 1924 SBC *Annual*, 22-23.
[70] 1925 SBC *Annual*, 18.
[71] 1926 SBC *Annual*, 17.
[72] 1927 SBC *Annual*, 18.

[73] 1928 SBC *Annual*, 15.

[74] 1929 SBC *Annual*, 17.

[75] 1930 SBC *Annual*, 18.

[76] 1931 SBC *Annual*, 17.

[77] 1932 SBC *Annual*, 17.

[78] Ibid., 72. This year began the tradition of electing a president to serve at the following year's meeting.

[79] 1933 SBC *Annual*, 44.

[80] 1934 SBC *Annual*, 84.

[81] 1935 SBC *Annual*, 44.

[82] 1936 SBC *Annual*, 64.

[83] 1937 SBC *Annual*, 79.

[84] 1938 SBC *Annual*, 65.

[85] 1939 SBC *Annual*, 58.

[86] 1940 SBC *Annual*, 53.

[87] 1941 SBC *Annual*, 64.

[88] 1942 SBC *Annual*, 50.

[89] 1944 SBC *Annual*, 70.

[90] 1946 SBC *Annual*, 76.

[91] 1947 SBC *Annual*, 45.

[92] 1948 SBC *Annual*, 48.

[93] 1949 SBC *Annual*, 45.

[94] 1950 SBC *Annual*, 54.

[95] 1951 SBC *Annual*, 49.

[96] 1952 SBC *Annual*, 45.

[97] 1953 SBC *Annual*, 47.

[98] 1954 SBC *Annual*, 47.

[99] 1955 SBC *Annual*, 43.

[100] 1956 SBC *Annual*, 51.

[101] 1957 SBC *Annual*, 57.

[102] 1958 SBC *Annual*, 57.

[103] 1959 SBC *Annual*, 58.

[104] 1960 SBC *Annual*, 60.

[105] 1961 SBC *Annual*, 76.

[106] 1962 SBC *Annual*, 64.

[107] 1963 SBC *Annual*, 64.

[108] 1964 SBC *Annual*, 67.

[109] 1965 SBC *Annual*, 78-79.

[110] 1966 SBC *Annual*, 86.

[111] 1967 SBC *Annual*, 58.

[112] 1968 SBC *Annual*, 66.

[113] 1969 SBC *Annual*, 78.

[114] 1970 SBC *Annual*, 64.

[115] 1971 SBC *Annual*, 61.

[116] 1972 SBC *Annual*, 71.

[117] 1973 SBC *Annual*, 73.

[118] 1974 SBC *Annual*, 68.

[119] 1975 SBC *Annual*, 57.

[120] 1976 SBC *Annual*, 40.

[121] 1977 SBC *Annual*, 39.

[122] 1978 SBC *Annual*, 45.

[123] 1979 SBC *Annual*, 43.

[124] 1980 SBC *Annual*, 40.

[125] 1981 SBC *Annual*, 43.

[126] 1982 SBC *Annual*, 48.

[127] 1983 SBC *Annual*, 39.

[128] 1984 SBC *Annual*, 44.

[129] 1985 SBC *Annual*, 73.

[130] 1986 SBC *Annual*, 61.

[131] 1987 SBC *Annual*, 53.

[132] 1988 SBC *Annual*, 61.

[133] 1989 SBC *Annual*, 45.

[134] 1990 SBC *Annual*, 56.

[135] 1991 SBC *Annual*, 42.

[136] 1992 SBC *Annual*, 81.

[137] 1993 SBC *Annual*, 52.

[138] 1994 SBC *Annual*, 96.

[139] 1995 SBC *Annual*, 64.

[140] 1996 SBC *Annual*, 74.

[141] 1997 SBC *Annual*, 60.

[142] 1998 SBC *Annual*, 66.

[143] 1999 SBC *Annual*, 81.

[144] 2000 SBC *Annual*, 70.

[145] 2001 SBC *Annual*, 65.

[146] 2002 SBC *Annual*, 69.

[147] 2003 SBC *Annual*, 63.

[148] 2004 SBC *Annual*, 76.

[149] 2005 SBC *Annual*, 97.

[150] 2006 SBC *Annual*, 89.

[151] 2007 SBC *Annual*, 75.

[152] 2008 SBC *Annual*, 77.

[153] 2009 SBC *Annual*, 78.

[154] 2010 SBC *Annual*, 101.

[155] 2011 SBC *Annual*, 86.

[156] 2012 SBC *Annual*, 71.

[157] 2013 SBC *Annual*, 70.

[158] 2014 SBC *Annual*, 68.

[159] 2015 SBC *Annual*, 71.

[160] 2016 SBC *Annual*, 93.

[161] 2017 SBC *Annual*, 71.

# Appendix B

# Cooperative Program Allocations by State

| State Convention | Percentage Allocated for State Ministries | Percentage Forwarded to SBC | |
|---|---|---|---|
| Alabama State Convention[1] | 50.00% | 50.00% | |
| Alaska Baptist Convention[2] | 63.00% | 37.00% | |
| Arizona Baptist Convention[3] | 68.00% | 32.00% | |
| Arkansas Baptist State Convention[4] | 56.23% | 43.77% | |
| California Southern Baptist Convention[5] | 65.00% | 35.00% | |
| Colorado Baptist General Convention[6] | 67.03% | 32.97% | |
| Dakota Baptist Convention[7] | 74% | 26% | |
| District of Columbia Baptist Convention[8] | Allows churches the opportunity of an undesignated giving plan with funding for SBC causes | | |
| Florida Baptist Convention[9] | 49.00% | 51.00% | |
| Georgia Baptist Convention[10] | 60.00% | 40.00% | . |

| | | | |
|---|---|---|---|
| Hawaii Pacific Baptist Convention[11] | 80% | 20% | |
| Illinois Baptist State Association[12] | 56.5% | 43.5% | |
| State Convention of Baptists in Indiana[13] | 60% | 40% | |
| Baptist Convention of Iowa[14] | 50.00% | 50.00% | |
| Kansas/Nebraska Convention of Southern Baptists[15] | 71.5% | 28.5% | Any budget excess is split 50/50 |
| Kentucky Baptist Convention[16] | 45.00% | 45.00% | 10.00% for Shared Ministry Expenses |
| Louisiana Baptist Convention[17] | 63.26% | 36.74% | |
| Baptist Convention of Maryland/Delaware[18] | 52.00% | 48% | |
| Baptist State Convention of Michigan[19] | 72.50% | 27.50% | |
| Minnesota/Wisconsin Baptist Convention[20] | 68.00% | 32.00% | |
| Mississippi Baptist Convention Board[21] | 62.5% | 37.5% | Any budget excess split 50/50 |
| Missouri Baptist Convention[22] | 60.00% | 40.00% | |
| Montana Southern Baptist Convention[23] | 75.00% | 25.00% | |
| Nevada Baptist Convention[24] | 50.00% | 50.00% | |
| Baptist Convention of New England[25] | 83.00% | 17.00% | |

| | | | |
|---|---|---|---|
| Baptist Convention of New Mexico[26] | 71.00% | 29.00% | 4.30% designated CP exempt (similar to shared ministry expenses) |
| Baptist Convention of New York[27] | 71% | 29% | |
| Baptist State Convention of North Carolina[28] | 59.00% | 41.00% | |
| Northwest Baptist Convention[29] | 72.75% | 27.25% | |
| State Convention of Baptists in Ohio[30] | 50.00% | 50.00% | |
| Baptist General Convention of Oklahoma[31] | 60.00% | 40.00% | |
| Baptist Convention of Pennsylvania/S. Jersey[32] | 72.5% | 27.5% | |
| Southern Baptist Convention of Puerto Rico and US Virgin Islands[33] | 89.90% | 10.10% | |
| South Carolina Baptist Convention[34] | 54.50% | 41.00% | 4.5% forwarded directly to IMB |
| Tennessee Baptist Convention[35] | 53.36% | 46.64% | |
| Baptist General Convention of Texas[36] | Allows churches to designate a national partner, with recommended (though not mandatory) 79/21 split | | |
| Southern Baptists of Texas Convention[37] | 45.00% | 55.00% | |
| Utah/Idaho Southern Baptist Convention[38] | 72.00% | 28.00% | |

| Baptist General Association of Virginia[39] | Allows churches to choose from customizable giving tracks, some of which include SBC causes | | |
|---|---|---|---|
| Southern Baptist Conservatives of Virginia[40] | 49.00% | 51.00% | 3.26% shared ministry expenses |
| West Virginia Convention of Southern Baptists[41] | 59.00% | 41.00% | |
| Wyoming Southern Baptist Mission Network[42] | 67.25% | 32.75% | |

(updated 2017)

[1] Alabama Baptist Staff, "Ala. Baptists spotlight CP, Samford relationship," Baptist Press, November 28, 2017, accessed December 4, 2017, http://www.bpnews.net/49967/ala-baptists-spotlight-cp-samford-relationship.

[2] Karen L. Willoughby, "Alaska Baptists celebrate outreach to highways, hedges," Baptist Press, October 5, 2017, accessed December 4, 2017, http://www.bpnews.net/49665/alaska-baptists-celebrate-outreach-to-highways-hedges.

[3] Elizabeth Yount, "Ariz. So. Baptists increase CP, report church planting," Baptist Press, November 28, 2017, accessed December 4, 2017, http://www.bpnews.net/49969/ariz-so-baptists-increase-cp-report-church-planting.

[4] Arkansas Baptist News Staff, "Ark. Baptists begin new CP formula for SBC causes," Baptist Press, November 27, 2017, accessed December 4, 2017, http://www.bpnews.net/49965/ark-baptists-begin-new-cp-formula-for-sbc-causes.

[5] Terry Barone and Holly Smith, "Calif. Baptists highlight 'The Power of One,'" Baptist Press, October 26, 2017, accessed December 4, 2017, http://www.bpnews.net/49794/calif-baptists-highlight-the-power-of-one.

[6] David Roach, "Colo. Baptists seek revival, anticipate building sale," Baptist Press, October 16, 2017, accessed December 4, 2017,

http://www.bpnews.net/49728/colo-baptists-seek-revival-anticipate -building-sale.

[7] Karen L. Willoughby, "Dakotas raise CP percentage, welcome new pastors," Baptist Press, September 29, 2017, accessed December 4, 2017, http://www.bpnews.net/49631/dakotas-raise-cp-percentage -welcome-new-pastors.

[8] Tammi Reed Ledbetter, "WRAP-UP: Over half states boost CP sending to SBC causes," Baptist Press, December 21, 2016, accessed December 4, 2017, http://www.bpnews.net/48089/wrapup-over-half -states-boost-cp-sending-to-sbc-causes.

[9] Keila Diaz and Nicole Kalil, "Sermon in Spanish marks a first for Fla. Convention," Baptist Press, December 1, 2017, accessed December 4, 2017, http://www.bpnews.net/49993/sermon-in-spanish -marks-a-first-for-fla-convention.

[10] Joe Westbury, "Ga. Baptists honor White; add college budget goals," Baptist Press, November 28, 2017, accessed December 4, 2017, http://www.bpnews.net/49968/ga-baptists-honor-white-add-college -budget-goals.

[11] David Roach, "Hawaii Baptists restructure budget, urge coop- eration," November 15, 2017, accessed December 4, 2017, http:// www.bpnews.net/49911/hawaii-baptists-restructure-budget-urge -cooperation.

[12] Meredith Flynn, Lisa Misner Sargent and Eric Reed, "Illinois churches prepare for new ministry frontiers," Baptist Press, November 21, 2017, accessed December 4, 2017, http://www.bpnews.net/49946 /illinois-churches-prepare-for-new-ministry-frontiers.

[13] SCBI & BP Staff, "Indiana Baptists meet at camp's new wor- ship center," Baptist Press, October 25, 2017, accessed December 4, 2017, http://www.bpnews.net/49776/indiana-baptists-meet-at-camps -new-worship-center.

[14] BCI Staff, "Iowa Baptists note church growth, increased giv- ing," Baptist Press, November 13, 2017, accessed December 4, 2017, http://www.bpnews.net/49890/iowa-baptists-note-church-growth -increased-giving.

[15] Eva Wilson/Baptist Digest, "Kan.-Neb. Baptists increase CP 1.5 percent," Baptist Press, October 25, 2017, accessed December 4,

2017, http://www.bpnews.net/49779/kanneb-baptists-increase-cp-15 -percent.

[16] Todd Deaton/Western Recorder, "Ky. Baptists urge evangelism, pledge to monitor CBF," Baptist Press, November 15, 2017, accessed December 4, 2017, http://www.bpnews.net/49913/ky-baptists-urge -evangelism-pledge-to-monitor-cbf.

[17] Brian Blackwell/Baptist Message, "La. Baptists urge prayer, 'aggressive going,'" Baptist Press, November 29, 2017, accessed December 4, 2017, http://www.bpnews.net/49975/la-baptists-urge -prayer-aggressive-going.

[18] Sharon Mager, "Md.-Del. Baptists raise CP budget 4.5% to SBC causes," Baptist Press, November 21, 2017, accessed December 4, 2017, http://www.bpnews.net/49944/mddel-baptists-raise-cp-budget -45-to-sbc-causes.

[19] David Roach, "Mich. Baptists pledge prayer for Sutherland Springs," Baptist Press, November 10, 2017, accessed December 4, 2017, http://www.bpnews.net/49888/mich-baptists-pledge-prayer-for -sutherland-springs.

[20] David Williams, "Minn.-Wis. churches elevate CP giving from 22 to 32%," Baptist Press, November 21, 2017, accessed December 4, 2017, http://www.bpnews.net/49938/minnwis-churches -elevate-cp-giving-from-22-to-32.

[21] William H. Perkins, Jr., "Miss. Baptists unanimous on 2018 budget of $31.4M," Baptist Press, November 14, 2017, accessed December 4, 2017, http://www.bpnews.net/49901/miss-baptists -unanimous-on-2018-budget-of-314m.

[22] Benjamin Hawkins/Missouri Pathway, "Mo. Baptists pursue synergy for transforming lives," Baptist Press, November 2, 2017, accessed December 4, 2017, http://www.bpnews.net/49835/mo-baptists -pursue-synergy-for-transforming-lives.

[23] Karen L. Willoughby, "Prayer, new partnerships highlight Montana conv.," Baptist Press, October 13, 2017, accessed December 4, 2017, http://www.bpnews.net/49721/prayer-new-partnerships-highlight -montana-conv.

[24] Karen L. Willoughby, "Nevada Baptists called 'pacesetter' for CP giving," Baptist Press, October 24, 2017, accessed December 4,

2017, http://www.bpnews.net/49771/nevada-baptists-called-pacesetter-for-cp-giving.

[25] Kimber Ross, "N.E. Baptists seek next generation, denounce racism," Baptist Press, November 13, 2017, accessed December 4, 2017, http://www.bpnews.net/49891/ne-baptists-seek-next-generation-denounce-racism.

[26] David Roach, "N.M. Baptists increase CP, hear Spanish sermon," Baptist Press, November 10, 2017, accepted December 4, 2017, http://www.bpnews.net/49885/nm-baptists-increase-cp-hear-spanish-sermon.

[27] BP Staff, "N.Y. Baptists add marriage, gender to constitution," Baptist Press, October 4, 2017, accessed December 4, 2017, http://www.bpnews.net/49654/ny-baptists-add-marriage-gender-to-constitution.

[28] BSC & Biblical Recorder Staff, "N.C. Baptists pray for revival, celebrate record CP support," Baptist Press, November 8, 2017, accessed December 4, 2017, http://www.bpnews.net/49867/nc-baptists-pray-for-revival-celebrate-record-cp-support.

[29] Cameron Crabtree, "NW Baptists' 70th meeting renews 'blessing' theme," Baptist Press, November 15, 2017, accessed December 4, 2017, http://www.bpnews.net/49907/nw-baptists-70th-meeting-renews-blessing-theme.

[30] SCBO & BP Staff, "Ohio Baptists hold to 50-50 SBC distribution," Baptist Press, November 30, 2017, accessed December 4, 2017, http://www.bpnews.net/49987/ohio-baptists-hold-to-5050-sbc-distribution.

[31] Chris Doyle, "Anthony Jordan delivers final address as BGCO exec," Baptist Press, November 17, 2017, accessed December 4, 2017, http://www.bpnews.net/49925/anthony-jordan-delivers-final-address-as-bgco-exec.

[32] Mark Sentell, "Pa./S. Jersey increases CP, launches simulcast," Baptist Press, November 15, 2017, accessed December 4, 2017, http://www.bpnews.net/49909/pas-jersey-increases-cp-launches-simulcast.

[33] http://www.sbc.net/cp/statecontributions/puertorico.asp.

[34] Butch Blume, "400 S.C. Baptists 'Unite' for citywide evangelism," Baptist Press, November 20, 2017, accessed December 4, 2017,

http://www.bpnews.net/49933/400-sc-baptists-unite-for-citywide
-evangelism.

[35] Lonnie Wilkey and David Dawson, "Tenn. Baptists adopt resolution against racism," Baptist Press, November 21, 2017, accessed December 4, 2017, http://www.bpnews.net/49945/tenn-baptists-adopt
-resolution-against-racism.

[36] Katie Lowrie, "BGCT 'Compelled' theme underscores living for Christ," Baptist Press, November 17, 2017, accessed December 4, 2017, http://www.bpnews.net/49916/bgct-compelled-theme-underscores
-living-for-christ.

[37] Staff/Southern Baptist Texan, "SBTC messengers encouraged in wake of Harvey, tragedy," Baptist Press, November 20, 2017, accessed December 4, 2017, http://www.bpnews.net/49932/sbtc
-messengers-encouraged-in-wake-of-harvey-tragedy.

[38] Karen L. Willoughby, "Utah-Idaho Baptists report numberic & financial gains," Baptist Press, October 25, 2017, accessed December 4, 2017, http://www.bpnews.net/49778/utahidaho-baptists-report-numeric
-and-financial-gains.

[39] Nathan White, "Responding to God's call focus of BGAV," Baptist Press, November 29, 2017, accessed December 4, 2017, http://
www.bpnews.net/49978/responding-to-gods-call-focus-of-bgav.

[40] SBC of Virginia Staff, "SBC Va. decries racism in Charlottesville resolution," Baptist Press, November 20, 2017, accessed December 4, 2017, http://www.bpnews.net/49931/sbc-va-decries-racism-in
-charlottesville-resolution.

[41] Cleve Persinger, "W.Va. Baptists 'all in,' tackle opoid crisis," Baptist Press, November 15, 2017, accessed December 4, 2017, http://
www.bpnews.net/49908/wva-baptists-all-in-tackle-opioid-crisis.

[42] Karen L. Willoughby, "Wyoming Baptists adopt new convention name," Baptist Press, November 8, 2017, accessed December 4, 2017, http://www.bpnews.net/49866/wyoming-baptists-adopt-new
-convention-name.

# Report of the Great Commission Resurgence Task Force[76]

## Penetrating the Lostness

Embracing a Vision for a Great Commission Resurgence among Southern Baptists

Final Report of the Great Commission Task Force of the Southern Baptist Convention

(as amended and adopted by the Southern Baptist Convention, June 16, 2010)

## Needed: A Great Commission Resurgence

In every generation, Southern Baptists have been called to reclaim our identity as a Great Commission movement of churches. Now is the time for this generation to answer the same call—to make an unconditional commitment to reach the nations for Christ, to plant and serve Gospel churches in

North America and around the world, and to mobilize Southern Baptists as a Great Commission people. Now is the time for a Great Commission Resurgence among Southern Baptists. A world of lostness is waiting—what are we waiting for?

## Assignment: A Great Commission Motion

In the 2009 meeting of the Southern Baptist Convention, messengers overwhelmingly adopted this motion:

> That the Southern Baptist Convention, meeting June 23–24, 2009, in Louisville, Kentucky, authorize the President of the Southern Baptist Convention to appoint a Great Commission Task Force charged to bring a report and any recommendations to the Southern Baptist Convention meeting in Orlando, Florida, June 15–16, 2010, concerning how Southern Baptists can work more faithfully and effectively together in serving Christ through the Great Commission.

President Johnny Hunt appointed a Great Commission Resurgence Task Force of twenty-two members, led by Ronnie Floyd of Northwest Arkansas as chairman. Over the last months, this Task Force has met both extensively and intensively, listening to Southern Baptists, evaluating the most urgent needs before us, and looking to the future with the call of Christ to the nations as our inspiration and passion.

We have been joined by thousands of prayer partners drawn from all over the world. We asked you, as Southern Baptists, to tell us what you see and to share your concerns. Southern Baptists from every sector of this Convention have talked to us, written to us, and prayed with us. We spent important hours listening to denominational leaders at every level, but we also spent much time listening to grassroots Southern Baptist church members, pastors, missionaries, church planters, and students. Southern Baptists have spoken, and we have been listening.

## Urgency: A World of Lostness

There are almost 7 billion human inhabitants of planet Earth. At the most generous estimate, somewhere around 1 billion are believing Christians. That means that over 6 billion people are lost, without Christ, and thus without hope. Of these 6 billion, over 3.5 billion have never heard the Gospel of Jesus Christ. Over 6,000 people groups are without any Christian witness. There is no way that Southern Baptists can make real progress toward reaching these unreached people groups unless we experience a genuine Great Commission Resurgence. We must see a tidal wave of evangelistic and missionary passion, or the numbers of unreached people groups will only grow, and lostness will spread.

In North America, evangelical Christians are falling behind the level of population growth. Put simply, we are failing to reach new immigrant populations, the teeming millions in urban areas, and a generation of youth and young adults who are living in a time of vast change and confused worldviews. Lostness is not only our concern when it is found across oceans—it must be our concern when it is across the street. North America represents a vast continent of lostness, where millions still have never heard the Gospel of Jesus Christ, and where many communities and ethnic groups are woefully underserved by Gospel churches.

In our own congregations, we see falling rates of baptism and other signs of concern. In 2008, Southern Baptist churches baptized more than 33,000 fewer people than in 1950—and that was with more than 17,000 additional churches. Baptism rates among teenagers have fallen dramatically, and many young people become disengaged with the church soon after graduation from high school. In 2008, we baptized only 75,000 teenagers. In 1972, we baptized 140,000. Why?

Research conducted by LifeWay Research on the Millennial generation and research by Thom Rainer on previous generations indicates that every American generation from early in the twentieth century forward has been less evangelized than generations before. Tracing generational patterns from the World War II generation to the Millennials, the estimated number of Christians has fallen from 65 percent to 15 percent. Churches in America are losing ground with each successive generation.

We desperately need to reach our communities for Christ— and this starts with our own young people. Furthermore, we must see this generation of young Baptists take their places on the front lines of the Great Commission Resurgence. Humanly speaking, that is our only hope for a bold advance of the Gospel in the coming generation.

## Reality: What Is Holding Us Back?

The Southern Baptist Convention came into being in 1845 in order to mobilize the energies of Southern Baptist churches for missions and evangelism. It is just that simple. Over the last 165 years, Southern Baptists have grown into a massive denomination, with over 40,000 churches and an international reach for the Gospel.

And yet, there are signs that Great Commission commitment is diminishing among us. While a passion for seeing the world reached for Christ cannot be reduced to a question of money, there is no way that we can reach the world without the resources that are necessary. Missionaries must be sent, churches must be planted, pastors must be trained, and a host of services must be made available.

But the average Southern Baptist gives only 2.5 percent of annual income to the local church and beyond. Does this reflect a Great Commission passion? Clearly not. We will never be able to push back against lostness at this level of giving.

Local Southern Baptist churches are now giving an average of 6 percent of annual receipts to the Cooperative Program. In other words, when Cooperative Program giving is reported, local congregations are retaining an average of 94 cents of every offering plate dollar. These contributions are vital and much appreciated, but there is no way the world will be reached for Christ at that level of congregational investment in missions.

Our state Baptist conventions are doing important work in reaching their own states for Christ, planting churches, educating young Christians, and partnering with other Baptists across the nation and around the world. But approximately 63 percent of all monies given through the Cooperative Program remains in the states—and the greatest percentage of these monies remains in the states with the largest Southern Baptist populations.

So much good work is being done. Many of our churches are growing, baptizing, and sending. Over the past two decades, Southern Baptist churches have learned to participate in missions in a whole new way—with tens of thousands of our church members going on mission trips and seeing a world of lostness with their own eyes. College and university students have been going, infusing a generation with new passion. State conventions are developing new ways of reaching North America, and local associations are devising new ways of linking churches together for ministry. On our seminary campuses, we see a generation of young Christians dissatisfied with business as usual—ready to risk themselves for the sake of the Gospel. Our mission boards report that Southern Baptists continue to answer the call, with candidates for service with the International Mission Board waiting for an opportunity to be deployed and church planters with the North American Mission Board ready and energized to plant Gospel churches. Throughout the Southern Baptist Convention, there are bright signs of promise and ample signs of hope.

So, what will it take to see a Great Commission Resurgence launched?

## Back to Basics: A Theology for Great Commission Faithfulness

A Great Commission Resurgence grows directly out of a Great Commission theology. Do we really believe that Jesus saves? Are we not united in the confidence that anyone who calls upon the name of the Lord will be saved? Are we not certain that the Gospel of Jesus Christ is the only message of salvation and that salvation is found in Christ alone? Are we not confirmed in our knowledge that every single believer is called to be a part of taking the Gospel to the nations? Do we not yearn to see the nations rejoice in the name of Jesus Christ? Do we not know that today is the acceptable day of salvation? If so, we will be ready to do whatever it takes to see a Great Commission Resurgence change our priorities, reshape our plans, and fuel our lives for God's glory.

The foundation for a Great Commission Resurgence is the truth of the Gospel.

We believe in order for us to work together more faithfully and effectively toward the fulfillment of the Great Commission, Southern Baptists need a renewed commitment to the Gospel of Jesus Christ, the message of missions and evangelism, the message that is found only in Jesus Christ and His atoning death for sinners. These are first and foremost.

This will mean that we recommit ourselves to sharing, proclaiming, and teaching this good news, as well as ministering and living in the power of the Gospel.

We call upon Southern Baptists to acknowledge the centrality of the Gospel message to everything we do and everything we are. We celebrate the great variety in Southern Baptist life, but we believe that our true unity can be found only in the good news of Jesus Christ. We call for a new focus on the primacy of the biblical Gospel.

We believe that every single person is a sinner, alienated from God and without hope apart from Christ. We are confident that God saves sinners by His grace and for His glory, and that our salvation is secured through the atoning life, death, and resurrection of our Lord Jesus Christ. We believe that salvation is given to all who come to a saving knowledge of Christ, trusting in Him and in Him alone for our salvation, the forgiveness of sins, and the gift of everlasting life. We declare to the whole world our belief that Jesus saves—this same Jesus who is the divine God-man, our substitutionary Savior, and reigning Lord, the Head of His church.

In Jesus Christ we place our trust and hope. In His Gospel we place our hope and ground our efforts for a Great Commission Resurgence in Southern Baptist life. While holding firmly to the promise that Christ will be with us to the end of the age, we seek faithfully to proclaim the Gospel to the nations.

We must also affirm the primacy and centrality of the local church in the life of the Southern Baptist Convention. The New Testament identifies the church as the central instrument of the Kingdom of God. We must return the local church to the primacy and centrality in the life and work of our denomination at every level.

At the same time, our churches need a new missional vision. The missional vision of the church is to present the Gospel of Jesus Christ to every person in the world and to make disciples of all the nations—nothing less.

Each individual congregation must accept the responsibility to reach their village, community, town, or city with the good news of Jesus Christ. Churches across the Southern Baptist Convention must envision afresh their calling to reach their region, their country, and the world with the Gospel of Jesus Christ. Every local church must operate as a missional strategy center, releasing and sending Christ followers to advance the Gospel regionally, nationally, and globally to penetrate the lostness in our world.

All of our Baptist work beyond the local church must exist solely to serve the local church in this mission. This is true for every Baptist association, state convention, and the Southern Baptist Convention. None of these exists for itself—all exist for the churches. Every pastor must be a missionary strategist, and every church must be a missionary sending center.

Every congregation exists to replicate itself and to plant other Gospel churches. Every entity of Baptist work must exist to serve our churches in this missional vision. Otherwise, a Great Commission Resurgence will never happen.

So, how can we make a Great Commission Resurgence happen? In truth, only God can bring this about. At the same time, our Lord has given this assignment to His church, and we are commanded to get to this work. The Great Commission is a command, not a suggestion.

# Component One: Getting the Mission Right

In order for us to work together more faithfully and effectively toward the fulfillment of the Great Commission, we ask Southern Baptists to adopt a new mission statement in order to focus our attention and direct our work toward a clear and compelling missional vision.

We believe that Southern Baptists will rally to a mission statement that offers a clear, concise, and deeply biblical vision of who we are and what we are to be about:

> As a convention of churches, our missional vision is to present the Gospel of Jesus Christ to every person in the world and to make disciples of all the nations.

Is this not who we are? Can we even think of settling for anything less? Our mission statement should be drawn directly from the words of Jesus. This missional vision must drive everything that Southern Baptists do, and reset every priority of the local church and the denomination.

If this is who we are, and what we know we must do, then let the whole world know that this is our mission.

*Thus, we will ask Southern Baptists to adopt this missional vision as a statement of what draws us together, establishes our purpose, and defines our passion before our churches and the watching world.*

## Component Two: Making Our Values Transparent

We must also work toward the creation of a new and healthy culture within the Southern Baptist Convention. If we are to grow together and work together in faithfulness to the command of Christ, we must establish a culture of trust, transparency, and truth among all Southern Baptists.

Thus, we ask Southern Baptists to embrace and adopt these Core Values:

### Christ-likeness

*We depend on the transforming power of the Holy Spirit, the Word of God, and prayer to make us more like Jesus Christ.*

### Truth

*We stand together in the truth of God's inerrant Word, celebrating the faith once for all delivered to the saints.*

### Unity

*We work together in love for the sake of the Gospel.*

### Relationships

*We consider others more important than ourselves.*

## Trust

*We tell one another the truth in love and do what we say we will do.*

## Future

*We value Southern Baptists of all generations and embrace our responsibility to pass this charge to a rising generation in every age, faithful until Jesus comes.*

## Local Church

*We believe the local church is given the authority, power, and responsibility to present the Gospel of Jesus Christ to every person in the world.*

## Kingdom

*We join other Christ-followers for the Gospel, the Kingdom of Christ, and the glory of God.*

***Thus, we will call Southern Baptists to embrace and adopt these Core Values as a means of ensuring that we work together in a way that will please our Lord and reflect our identity as fellow believers in service to the Lord Jesus Christ.***

# Component Three: Encouraging Cooperative Program Giving and Other Great Commission Giving

A Great Commission Resurgence will require a new level of sacrificial giving from Southern Baptist church members and congregations. At the center of our funding stands the Cooperative Program, which since 1925 has served to mobilize the stewardship of Southern Baptists for worldwide missions and ministry.

We call upon Southern Baptists to reclaim our core identity as churches on mission, working together to take the Gospel to the nations and to fulfill our mandate as a Great Commission fellowship of churches. Our work together must be undergirded by cooperative investment in these tasks. We call upon Southern Baptists to honor and affirm the Cooperative Program as the most effective means of mobilizing our churches and extending our reach. We also call upon Southern Baptists to celebrate all giving to our common work. We will recognize the total of all monies channeled through the causes of the Southern Baptist Convention, the state conventions, and associations as Great Commission Giving. The greatest stewardship of Great Commission investment and deployment is giving through the Cooperative Program. We call upon Southern Baptists to recommit to the Cooperative Program as the central and preferred conduit of Great Commission funding, without which we would be left with no unified and cooperative strategy and commitment to the Great Commission task. We are a Great Commission people who are called to sacrificial and increasing giving, that the peoples of the earth may know the salvation that comes through faith in Jesus Christ alone.

Furthermore, we recognize that our national mission offerings are indispensable conduits for Great Commission funding. Therefore, we call upon Southern Baptists to adopt goals of giving no less than $200 million annually through the Lottie Moon Christmas Offering for International Missions and $100 million annually through the Annie Armstrong Easter Offering for North American Missions by 2015.

We reaffirm the definition of the Cooperative Program adopted by action of the 2007 Southern Baptist Convention. We honor and affirm the Cooperative Program as the most effective and efficient means of channeling the sacrificial support of our churches through undesignated giving, which funds both the state conventions and the work of the Southern Baptist Convention. We call upon the churches of the Southern Baptist Convention to increase the percentage of their Cooperative Program giving.

We call upon the state conventions to increase the percentage of Cooperative Program funds directed to the Southern Baptist Convention.

We call upon every entity of the Southern Baptist Convention to maximize all Cooperative Program funds for the task of taking the Gospel to the nations and serving Great Commission churches in their fulfillment of this mandate.

We call upon all Southern Baptists to celebrate every dollar given by faithful Southern Baptists as part of Great Commission Giving, including designated gifts given to any Baptist association, state convention, and to the causes of the Southern Baptist Convention.

We call upon Southern Baptists to evaluate every budget, from the budget of the individual Southern Baptist church member to the budgets of the Southern Baptist Convention and its entities, in terms of a Great Commission focus and commitment.

We call upon Southern Baptists to exercise the stewardship of wealth for the Great Commission through estate planning and planned gifts that will undergird the work of the Great Commission long after we have departed this life.

*Thus, we will call upon Southern Baptists to give as never before, to support the Cooperative Program as never before, and to celebrate every church's eager and sacrificial support of Great Commission Giving at every level.*

# Component Four: Reaching North America

As we listened to Southern Baptists, the mission of reaching North America with the Gospel was a clear concern and priority. This was a concern shared by leaders of the North American Mission Board as they met with us in the course of our work. The central concern of all was the priority of liberating NAMB to conduct and direct a strategy of reaching the United States and Canada with the Gospel and planting Gospel churches.

Thus, we believe that the North American Mission Board must be refocused and unleashed for greater effectiveness. Therefore, we call upon Southern Baptists to affirm NAMB with a priority to plant churches in North America, reach our cities and underserved regions and people groups, and clarify its role to lead and accomplish efforts to reach North America with the Gospel.

The North American Mission Board of the Southern Baptist Convention exists to penetrate lostness throughout North America by assisting Southern Baptist churches in their task of reaching North America with the Gospel of Jesus Christ through ministries of evangelism, church planting, and to mobilize Southern Baptist churches as a missional movement. How will this be done?

This reinvention of the North American Mission Board that we envision will implement a missional strategy for planting churches in North America with a priority to reach metropolitan areas and underserved people groups. We desire for the North American Mission Board to encourage Southern Baptist churches to become church planting congregations. Regardless of the size or location of our churches, we call for each to have a vision for planting churches somewhere in North America. It is our desire that at least 50 percent of the ministry efforts of our North American Mission Board be given to assist churches in planting healthy, multiplying, and faithful Baptist congregations in the United States and Canada.

We also call for NAMB to reclaim its mission of assisting churches to make disciples, working with LifeWay Christian Resources and other partners. Our churches are in great need of leadership, strategies, and materials for making disciples. We believe that NAMB is best suited to fulfill this leadership mission for the Southern Baptist Convention.

Similarly, we call for NAMB to be prioritized with the task of leadership development through the development of current pastoral leadership, with particular attention to contextual evangelism and church planting. NAMB must become a central engine for building missional momentum among Southern Baptist pastors.

If we are going to reach the 258 million lost people in the United States and Canada, we must address the fact that the vast majority of our Cooperative Program mission funds devoted to North America are expended in the most evangelized regions of our work. Approximately two-thirds of our Cooperative Program dollars are spent on regions where only one-third of the population resides. In other words, the greatest percentage of mission funds remains where our own churches are concentrated.

We call upon NAMB to penetrate lostness in partnership with state conventions located in the most unreached and underserved populations of North America.

Our hope and vision is to see NAMB reprioritized, decentralized, and fully authorized to lead Southern Baptists in this great work. This will mean the phasing out of Cooperative Agreements, a structure in place since the 1950s, that return a tremendous percentage of CP monies back to the regions where Southern Baptists are most greatly concentrated and often leaves NAMB with insufficient mobility to appoint personnel directly and ensure missional focus.

We recognize that in order to accomplish its mission for Southern Baptists, NAMB must work in partnership with the state conventions, and we affirm the need for this partnership to be based in cooperation and basic agreement concerning strategies. Nevertheless, we are convinced that the Cooperative Agreements must be replaced with a more appropriate structure and pattern of cooperation. Thus, we call for the leadership of the North American Mission Board to budget for a national strategy that will mobilize Southern Baptists in a great effort to reach North America with the Gospel and plant thriving, reproducing churches. We encourage NAMB to set a goal of phasing out all Cooperative Agreements within seven years, and to establish a new pattern of strategic partnership with the state conventions that will penetrate lostness and ensure greater responsiveness to the Southern Baptist Convention and greater effectiveness for NAMB in the appointment of missionary personnel and church planters.

*Thus, we will ask Southern Baptists to unleash the North American Mission Board for a new era of leadership and service to Southern Baptists, pushing back against the lostness of the United States and Canada.*

APPENDIX C

# Component Five: Reaching Unreached and Underserved People Groups within North America

When the Southern Baptist Convention was founded, the world was rather easily divided into "home" and "foreign" missions. That world is gone. Now, with revolutions in transportation and the movement of peoples, the world has come to North America. Indeed, some of the largest concentrations of populations of unreached and underserved people groups are found within the world's so-called international cities. Beyond this, significant populations of these people groups are now found even in smaller communities, especially those with colleges and universities.

At present, the mission statement of the International Mission Board prevents active involvement in mission efforts within North America. We believe that restriction fits the past far better than the present, much less the future. The International Mission Board has the charge to develop strategies for reaching these unreached and underserved people groups around the world, and this most often means a deep involvement in language and cultural studies. We need to allow the IMB to utilize those skills and that knowledge within North America as well. Put simply, it makes no sense to duplicate this effort and work with an artificial separation of the mission. Mission strategists estimate that there may be as many as 586 unreached and underserved people groups with representation within the United States. Many of these people groups are already within the reach of the International Mission Board, with personnel developing strategies based in their language and culture. We must take advantage of the expertise of both of our mission boards where it is most needed—working in coordination in order to make the greatest impact for the Great Commission.

Thus, such efforts must be done in communication with the North American Mission Board. This proposal has been thoroughly considered with NAMB leadership, and we are fully confident that these two mission boards can and will serve Southern Baptists and maximize their combined reach by working together in reaching these unreached and underserved people groups where they are found in North America. The North American Mission Board retains the leadership mission of reaching North America with the Gospel. We are encouraged to know that a spirit of cooperation already exists between the boards on this very issue.

*Thus, we will ask Southern Baptists to entrust to the International Mission Board the ministry of reaching unreached and underserved people groups without regard to any geographic limitation.*

## Component Six: Promoting the Cooperative Program and Elevating Stewardship

There can be no question that Southern Baptists must prioritize the promotion of the Cooperative Program and the elevation of stewardship among our churches. The 1995 "Covenant for a New Century" reorganization of the Convention assigned Cooperative Program promotion to the Executive Committee of the Southern Baptist Convention. Later, stewardship education was added as a ministry assignment.

We believe that the state conventions must take the lead in both ministries. In essence, this is how the Cooperative Program began. As Albert McClellan, author of the official history of the Executive Committee noted, "It was understood from the beginning that state conventions should be responsible for promoting the Cooperative Program in the field and gathering the funds from the churches."[77]

The reason for this is straightforward and easy to see. The state conventions have the mechanisms in place to collect funds and promote the Cooperative Program. This has been their historic role and continuing passion.

Clearly, there must also be a role for the Southern Baptist Convention. The Cooperative Program is a partnership, and both the SBC and the state conventions have important work to do. This means an important and continuing leadership role for the SBC Executive Committee as well.

*We strongly encourage the Executive Committee of the Southern Baptist Convention to work with the state conventions, charged with the responsibility of Cooperative Program and stewardship education, in developing a strategy for encouraging our churches to greater participation and investment in the Cooperative Program. This is an immediate need, made more urgent by the rise of a new generation of Southern Baptists, ready for leadership and deployment in service to the Great Commission. Our hope is that a unified strategy with clearly established goals will be in place by the meeting of the Southern Baptist Convention in 2013.*

# Component Seven: The Call of the Nations and the SBC Allocation Budget

For many years, Southern Baptists have been proud of the fact that 50 percent of all Cooperative Program funds received by the Southern Baptist Convention are distributed to the International Mission Board. Thus, we are able to say that half of all Cooperative Program receipts at the national level go to international missions.

While this is a matter of genuine and understandable denominational pride, it has become too comfortable. It is time to increase that percentage above 50 percent.

We recognize that Southern Baptists are rightly committed to a full range of denominational programs, ministries, and mission efforts. The strength of the Cooperative Program is its reach and comprehensiveness, and for this we are thankful.

At the same time, we will never reach the world while staying in a position of denominational comfort. Therefore, it is our hope to see Southern Baptists break the "50 percent barrier" and make a bold statement of our present and future commitment to reach the nations with the Gospel.

*We ask Southern Baptists to support this goal by affirming an intention to raise the Cooperative Program SBC Allocation Budget percentage received by the International Mission Board to 51 percent. Further, we ask that Southern Baptists affirm the intention to fund this increase through a reduction in the budget granted to Facilitating Ministries, thus making a statement about our commitment to reduce denominational infrastructure in order to set the pace for growth in commitment to reaching the nations.*

# Conclusion

The components of our report do not represent a revolution in Southern Baptist life and work. Our Task Force was given several months in which to look at the most urgent issues among us, and to find ways that will allow Southern Baptists to work more faithfully and effectively together in serving Christ through the Great Commission.

We have come to the conclusion that these specific components will make a real difference, even as we recognize that these are only a start. This report must represent the beginning of a new spirit of Great Commission commitment and prioritization, not the end.

Therefore, at the conclusion of this report we bring a series of challenges that will reach every Southern Baptist church and church member, along with every level of Southern Baptist work and every entity of the Convention. We recognize that the challenge of working toward a Great Commission Resurgence will require the commitment of a generation, not merely of the messengers to an annual meeting of the Southern Baptist Convention.

Nevertheless, we are confident that these components are of vital importance to the future of our denomination and its work—and are key to making immediate progress toward a Great Commission Resurgence.

We must keep ever in mind the command that frames the very reason for our existence:

> Then Jesus came near and said to them, "All authority has been given to Me in heaven and on earth. Go, therefore, and make disciples of all nations, baptizing them

in the name of the Father and of the Son and of the Holy Spirit, teaching them to observe everything I have commanded you. And remember, I am with you always, to the end of the age." (Matthew 28:18–20, Holman Christian Standard Bible)

May God bring glory to His name and the redeeming power of the Gospel of Christ through granting to Southern Baptists in this generation what can only be described as a Great Commission Resurgence.

A world of lostness awaits. What are we waiting for?

## Recommendations to the Southern Baptist Convention

1. That the messengers to the Southern Baptist Convention, meeting in Orlando, Florida, June 15–16, 2010, adopt the following as the mission statement of the Southern Baptist Convention:

   > As a Convention of churches, our missional vision is to present the Gospel of Jesus Christ to every person in the world and to make disciples of all the nations.

2. That the messengers to the Southern Baptist Convention, meeting in Orlando, Florida, June 15–16, 2010, adopt the following as Core Values for our work together:

   > **Christ-likeness**—We depend on the transforming power of the Holy Spirit, the Word

of God, and prayer to make us more like Jesus Christ.

**Truth**—We stand together in the truth of God's inerrant Word, celebrating the faith once for all delivered to the saints.

**Unity**—We work together in love for the sake of the Gospel.

**Relationships**—We consider others more important than ourselves.

**Trust**—We tell one another the truth in love and do what we say we will do.

**Future**—We value Southern Baptists of all generations and embrace our responsibility to pass this charge to a rising generation in every age, faithful until Jesus comes.

**Local Church**—We believe the local church is given the authority, power, and responsibility to present the Gospel of Jesus Christ to every person in the world.

**Kingdom**—We join other Christ-followers for the Gospel, the Kingdom of Christ, and the glory of God.

3. That the messengers to the Southern Baptist Convention, meeting in Orlando, Florida, June 15–16, 2010, request the Executive Committee of the Southern Baptist Convention to consider recommending to the Southern Baptist

Convention the adoption of the language and structure of Great Commission Giving as described in this report in order to enhance and celebrate the Cooperative Program and the generous support of Southern Baptists channeled through their churches, and to continue to honor and affirm the Cooperative Program as the most effective means of mobilizing our churches and extending our outreach. We affirm that designated gifts to special causes are to be given as a supplement to the Cooperative Program and not as a substitute for Cooperative Program giving. We further request that the boards of trustees of the International Mission Board and North American Mission Board, in consultation with the Woman's Missionary Union, consider the adoption of the Lottie Moon and Annie Armstrong offering goals as outlined in this report.

4.  That the messengers to the Southern Baptist Convention, meeting June 15–16, 2010, request the Executive Committee of the Southern Baptist Convention to consider any revision to the ministry assignment of the North American Mission Board that may be necessary in order to accomplish the redirection of NAMB as outlined in this report; and that the board of trustees of the North American Mission Board be asked to consider the encouragements found within this report in all matters under their purview.

5.  That the messengers to the Southern Baptist Convention, meeting June 15–16, 2010, request that the Executive Committee of the Southern Baptist Convention and the International Mission Board of the Southern Baptist Convention consider a revised ministry assignment for

the International Mission Board that would remove any geographical limitation on its mission to reach unreached and underserved people groups wherever they are found.

6. That the messengers to the Southern Baptist Convention, meeting June 15–16, 2010, request the Executive Committee of the Southern Baptist Convention to consider working with the leadership of the state conventions in developing a comprehensive program of Cooperative Program promotion and stewardship education in alignment with this report.

7. That the messengers to the Southern Baptist Convention, meeting June 15–16, 2010, in Orlando, Florida, request the Executive Committee of the Southern Baptist Convention to consider recommending an SBC Cooperative Program Allocation Budget that will increase the percentage allocated to the International Mission Board to 51 percent by decreasing the Executive Committee's percentage of the SBC Allocation Budget by 1 percent.

# Challenges Addressed to All Southern Baptists

We hold to an ecclesiology that honors and affirms both autonomy and cooperation. The Great Commission Resurgence Task Force is well aware of this, and we realize that we cannot direct individual Christians, local churches, associations or state conventions to take any particular or specific action. This is as it should be. However, our doctrine of the church does not prevent us from challenging, encouraging, admonishing, and advising one another at all levels of SBC life for greater passion and effectiveness in pursuing the Great Commission. We are a Convention of churches with a missional vision to present the Gospel of Jesus Christ to every person in the world and to make disciples of all the nations. With all of this in mind, we wish to put forth the following as challenges for the future of the SBC that we might bring greater glory to the Lord Jesus as we seek to disciple all nations in the fulfillment of Matthew 28:18–20.

## Challenges for Individual Christians

- Return to God in deep repentance of and brokenness over sin, denying self, and coming to God with complete humility.
- Commit to the total and absolute Lordship of Jesus Christ in every area of your life, understanding that Christ's Lordship is inseparable from all aspects of the believer's life, including family obligations, business and profession, and recreational or leisure pursuits. We especially call on men to respond to this challenge.
- Devote yourself to a radical pursuit of the Great Commission in the context of obeying the Great Commandments of loving God and loving others.
- Participate in a local church sponsored evangelism training class sometime during 2011 and make this a regular component of the discipleship process in your life.
- Develop strategies as an individual for praying for, serving, sharing the Gospel [with] and discipling neighbors, coworkers, and others with whom you come into regular contact.

- Bear witness to the Gospel through personal evangelism, seeing every individual as a sinner in need of the salvation that comes through Jesus Christ alone.
- Participate in a North American or international mission trip sponsored by your church or association at least once every four years.
- Grow in giving as a faithful financial steward with at least 10 percent of your income going to your local church. However, see 10 percent as a place to begin in grace giving but not the place to stop.
- Determine to exercise a greater level of stewardship through estate planning and planned giving, leaving a percentage of your estate to your local church, the Cooperative Program, and to a faithful Baptist entity such as NAMB, IMB, a Baptist college, or our seminaries.
- Give serious consideration to adoption and orphan care as a component of Great Commission living.
- Determine to develop a well-rounded Christian worldview that allows you to clearly articulate both what you believe and why you believe.
- Repent of any and all sin that has prevented you from being fully used by our Lord in fulfilling the Great Commission. This includes sins of idolatry, pride, selfish ambition, hatred, racism, bigotry and other sins of the flesh that dishonor the name of Jesus.

## Challenges for Individual Families

- Emphasize biblical gender roles with believing fathers taking the lead in modeling Great Commission

Christianity and taking the primary responsibility for the spiritual welfare of their families.

- Recognize that parents have the primary responsibility of educating their children and helping them to cultivate a Christian worldview way of thinking and living.

- Build Gospel saturated homes that see children as a gift from God and our initial mission field. Consider, in this context, the vital ministries of adoption and orphan care.

- Make prayer for and the evangelism and discipleship of children a family priority that begins with parents and is assisted by local churches.

- Develop strategies as a family for praying for, serving, and sharing the Gospel with neighbors, coworkers, and others with whom family members come into regular contact.

- Adopt a different unreached people group each month and pray as a family 1) for IMB missionaries working with the people group, 2) for the conversion, baptism, and discipling of countless individuals within the people group, and 3) for the establishment of biblical churches among the people group.

- Adopt a different North American church plant each month and pray as a family 1) for the church's leadership team, 2) for the conversion, baptism, and discipling of countless individuals in the church's region, and 3) for the birthing of future church plants from the church.

- Spend a family vacation participating in a local church or association sponsored mission trip.

- Consider setting up a missions savings account for each of your children that would enable them to spend six months to a year in a North American or international missions context soon after graduating from high school.

## Challenges for Local Churches and Pastors

- Lead your church by calling a Solemn Assembly in January 2011 for the purpose of calling Christ's people to return to God, to repentance, and to humility in service to a renewed commitment to Christ and the Great Commission. We request that the newly elected President of the Southern Baptist Convention lead Southern Baptists in this effort.

- Become knowledgeable of the mission field of your specific region, identifying the various people groups and developing a strategy to penetrate the lostness in your region. Be intentional in working with your local association, state convention, and NAMB in pursuing this task.

- Work to cultivate a Great Commission atmosphere that is contagious in your church and becomes the DNA of the pastor, staff, adults, students, youth, and children of your local body of Christ.

- Working with the IMB and NAMB, set goals for Lottie Moon and Annie Armstrong that will enable us to send $200 million to the IMB and $100 million to NAMB in annual gifts by 2015.

- Strengthen mission education for believers of all ages, working with the Woman's Missionary Union and other missions education programs. Every believer must be made aware of the global missions challenge.

- Lead your church to grow and increase in sacrificial Cooperative Program giving.
- Make sure every sermon, devotion, or other type of teaching is Gospel centered and driven by the inerrant and infallible text of Scripture with emphasis on how to apply the text to the lives of different kinds of people.
- Make sure every sermon, devotion, or other type of teaching clearly articulates and applies the Gospel message and is centered in the grand narrative of Scripture.
- Call your people continually to a radical devotion and surrender to the Lordship of Jesus Christ.
- Preach passionately for the conversion of the lost and extend consistently the Gospel call for persons to be saved.
- Honor the role of the evangelist, affirming the calling and witness of those who give their lives to the call of the Gospel.
- Challenge people to identify with Christ and testify to Him through believer's baptism by immersion.
- Call people passionately and consistently to surrender their lives to full-time ministry. Include in this call the challenge to a career as a missionary through the IMB or NAMB.
- Preach regularly and passionately on Christian stewardship, helping your people see this as a vital component of discipleship and life lived under the Lordship of Jesus Christ. Undergird this with lessons on biblical stewardship in your church's Bible study ministries.
- Cultivate an atmosphere of evangelism, missions, discipleship, and biblical theology that permeates every aspect of the church's ministry.

- Give particular attention to the evangelizing and discipling of children and youth.
- Get involved in a regular church-planting program at some level of your congregation's capability. This can include specific partnerships with another church, your association, state convention, or NAMB.
- Adopt an unreached people group and an underserved megacity in North America and regularly inform the membership about them, pray for them, and when applicable, work toward short-term mission trips to serve them. Encourage families to consider moving to those cities to be part of the core group for that plant.
- Plan at least one evangelism training course annually for your church members; consider inviting members of other churches in your association to participate, especially smaller churches.
- Plan at least one North American or international mission trip a year and/or encourage members to participate in mission trips sponsored by a local association.
- Develop a comprehensive strategy for sharing the Gospel with every person in your community with no regard to racial, social, or economic status. This may include elements such as home-to-home evangelism, neighborhood block parties, servant evangelism projects, one-on-one mentoring, after-school programs, university campus outreach, innovative outreach events, neighborhood Bible studies, evangelistic mercy ministries, etc.
- Enter, if possible, the world of private Christian schooling and Christian homeschooling to provide a Christian alternative for the education of children, especially in

areas hostile to the Christian worldview. See this as a complement to the many faithful Christians serving in the public school systems who see their calling to be salt and light in a missional assignment.

- Encourage Christian schools to send each student in their high school years on a crosscultural missions experience or to an international mission field for at least one week before they graduate, developing a strategy to pay for these trips as a school in order to build a genuine passion and commitment to reach the nations.
- Develop a comprehensive strategy for Great Commission discipling of all church members. This may include elements such as Sunday school and/or small group ministries, mission education programs, one-on-one mentoring, affinity ministries (e.g., women, singles, etc.), pastoral leadership training, diaconal leadership training, etc.
- Develop a comprehensive church-based strategy for reaching and discipling college students, including international students.
- Develop a comprehensive church-based strategy for reaching and discipling individuals with physical and developmental disabilities.
- Send teenagers and young adults on mission trips with the hope of exposing every young believer to global missions.
- Partner with like-minded ethnic churches or missions in evangelizing immigrants and other underserved ethnic minorities, including migrants and other short-term workers.

- Reclaim the Baptist vision of regenerate church membership, recognizing that this vision is central to our Baptist identity and understanding of the church.
- Reclaim corrective church discipline as the biblical means of restoring believers to healthy discipleship and faithfulness.
- Emphasize meaningful church membership through such practices as decision counseling, believer's baptism, new convert mentoring, membership covenants, prospective member classes, and redemptive church discipline.

## Challenges for Local Associations

- Enthusiastically embrace the missional vision and core values of the SBC, allowing them to guide your work and set your priorities.
- Adopt the Baptist Faith and Message (2000) as your confessional basis of association and adopt some shared core values and priorities that characterize the cooperating churches of your association.
- Organize quarterly associational prayer meetings for the conversion of the lost and the planting of sound churches in the underserved and unreached areas of North America and around the globe.
- Work with state Conventions and the SBC to set aside January of every year as a month of prayer for the conversion of unreached people groups around the globe.
- Plan at least one annual foreign mission trip and one annual North American mission trip and encourage all

the churches in the association to participate, especially smaller churches.

- Develop associational collections of evangelism and discipleship resources and regularly inform the churches about the availability of such resources.
- Work with cooperating churches to plant at least one new church a year in an underserved area within or near the association.
- Work with cooperating churches to plan at least one mercy ministry focused outreach event every year.

## Challenges for State Conventions

- Embrace with enthusiasm the missional vision and core values of the SBC, allowing them to guide your work and set your priorities.
- Adopt the Baptist Faith and Message (2000) as a confessional basis for cooperation and adopt shared core values and priorities that characterize cooperating churches.
- Make church planting a priority and develop church planting partnerships with North American urban centers and underserved regions outside of the Southeast and Southwest.
- Determine to return to the historic ideal of a 50/50 Cooperative Program distribution between the state conventions and the SBC, recognizing the historic commitment of the SBC and the state conventions to share expenses for the promotion and administration of the Cooperative Program.
- Hold state convention colleges and universities accountable to Baptist convictions and an authentic Christian

worldview education. Baptist colleges and universities must inculcate a Great Commission mind-set in their students and deploy them worldwide in short-term missionary service.

- Eliminate programs that do not directly assist local churches in fulfilling their biblical mandate to make disciples of all people.
- Work with the SBC and local associations to set aside January of every year as a month of prayer for the conversion of unreached people groups around the globe.
- Work with local associations and local churches to plan regional evangelism and discipleship training events on at least a semiannual basis.
- Encourage state convention children's homes to consider deep investment in Great Commission adoption/foster ministries that connect children with Baptist families within the state.
- Recognize the powerful witness of disaster relief programs as Southern Baptists have touched millions of lives in the aftermath of disaster and in a moment of acute need.
- Develop and celebrate mercy ministries which can be used as avenues for churches to serve others and open doors for evangelism.

## Challenges for LifeWay

- Create materials that our churches can use to teach biblical stewardship through our Sunday schools and other Bible study ministries.

- Create materials our churches can use to teach personal evangelism and the call to each Christian to be involved in fulfilling the Great Commission. Create a simple but biblically rooted disciple-making plan that helps pastors and leaders to multiply themselves.
- Develop materials that assist individuals in their understanding and involvement in the Great Commission, both in North America and in the world.
- Strengthen ministries directed to the support of Christian schools and homeschooling families.

## Challenges for the Seminaries

- Remember never to lose sight that your calling is to serve the churches of the SBC.
- Maintain fidelity to our confession of faith (the Baptist Faith and Message [2000]).
- Train and send to our churches Great Commission ministers who will lead us in becoming Great Commission churches.
- Develop a strategy for cultivating more local church-based partnerships for MDiv-level theological education, particularly in underserved regions in North America.
- Develop more opportunities for students to gain tangible experience and earn seminary credit by serving in local church internships or short-term mission assignments and provide financial assistance to students who avail themselves of these opportunities.
- Give primary attention to master's and doctoral-level programs for the education and training of pastors, missionaries, and other church leaders.

- Train students in the skills of disciple-making, affirming this calling as central to the task of the minister.

- Develop programs of study (and host regular conferences and workshops) that are specifically geared toward equipping local church leadership (both students and nonstudents) in areas such as preaching, evangelism, discipleship, pastoral ministries, church planting, international missions, and biblical counseling, etc.

- Cooperate with local associations, state conventions, NAMB, and the IMB in planning and hosting church planting training that puts international missions and church planting in the life-blood of all the students our churches entrust to your care.

## Challenge for the Ethics and Religious Liberty Commission

- Renew efforts to call upon God's people to live and demonstrate Christ-likeness and moral witness as an example and testimony for Jesus Christ and continue efforts to preserve religious freedom in our nation so that the Gospel of Jesus Christ can be proclaimed and the Great Commission fulfilled.

## Challenge for GuideStone Financial Resources

- Mobilize those who are retired and receiving benefits to use their energy in praying for and becoming personally involved in the evangelization of North America and the world.

## Challenges to All Southern Baptist Leaders

- Take advantage of every opportunity to support the Cooperative Program among Southern Baptists and Southern Baptist churches.
- Enhance confidence in all Southern Baptist work by honoring the Business and Financial Plan of the Southern Baptist Convention.
- Commit to a continuous process of denominational review in order to ensure maximum implementation of the Great Commission.

# The Great Commission Task Force of the Southern Baptist Convention

**Johnny Hunt**—SBC President, Ex-officio member of the GCR Task Force, Senior Pastor of First Baptist Church, Woodstock, GA

**Ronnie Floyd**—GCR Task Force Chairman, Senior Pastor of First Baptist Church of Springdale and The Church at Pinnacle Hills, AR

**Daniel Akin**—President, Southeastern Baptist Theological Seminary, Wake Forest, NC

**Tom Biles**—Executive Director, Tampa Bay Baptist Association, FL

**John Cope**—Senior Pastor of Keystone Community Fellowship, Chalfont, PA

**David Dockery**—President, Union University, Jackson, TN

**John Drummond**—Owner, DMG Development, Panama City, FL

**Donna Gaines**—Women's Communicator, Pastor's Wife, Bellevue Baptist Church, Cordova, TN

**Al Gilbert**—Senior Pastor, Calvary Baptist Church, Winston-Salem, NC

**Larry Grays**—Senior Pastor, Midtown Bridge Church, Atlanta, GA

**J. D. Greear**—Lead Pastor, The Summit Church, Durham, NC

**Ruben Hernandez**—Vocational Evangelist, Plano, TX

**Harry Lewis**—Vice President of Partnership, Missions, and Mobilization Group at NAMB, GA

**Kathy Ferguson Litton**—Women's Communicator, Pastor's Wife, First Baptist North Mobile, AL

**Albert Mohler, Jr.**—President, The Southern Baptist Theological Seminary, Louisville, KY

**Mike J. Orr**—Pastor, First Baptist Church, Chipley, FL

**Jim Richards**—Executive Director, Southern Baptists of Texas Convention, TX

**Roger Spradlin**—Senior Pastor, Valley Baptist Church, Bakersfield, CA

**Ted H. Traylor**—Pastor, Olive Baptist Church, Pensacola, FL

**Simon Tsoi**—Executive Director, Chinese Baptist Fellowship of the U.S. and Canada, AZ

**Robert White**—Executive Director, Georgia Baptist Convention, GA

**Ken Whitten**—Senior Pastor, Idlewild Baptist Church, Lutz, FL

# NOTES

1. Southern Baptist Convention Constitution, Article II.
2. Southern Baptist Convention Constitution, Preamble.
3. Southern Baptist Convention Charter.
4. Robert G. Gardner, *A Decade of Debate and Division: Georgia Baptists and the Formation of the Southern Baptist Convention* (Macon, GA: Mercer University Press, 1995), 13–16.
5. Ibid.
6. "Resolution on Racial Reconciliation on the 150th Anniversary of the Southern Baptist Convention," passed by the 1995 Southern Baptist Convention.
7. Henry M. Robert et al., *Robert's Rules of Order*, 11th ed. (Philadelphia: Da Capo Press, 2011), 7.
8. Southern Baptist Convention Bylaw 1.
9. Bill Leonard, *Baptist Ways: A History* (Valley Forge, PA: Judson Press, 2003), 92.
10. James L. Sullivan, *Baptist Polity as I See It* (Nashville: Broadman Press, 1983), 156.
11. Southern Baptist Convention Constitution, Article III.
12. Southern Baptist Convention Bylaw 8.
13. Southern Baptist Convention Constitution, Article III.
14. Southern Baptist Convention Constitution, Article IV.
15. Southern Baptist Convention Constitution, Article V.
16. Southern Baptist Convention Bylaw 19.
17. Southern Baptist Convention Bylaw 20.
18. Southern Baptist Convention Bylaw 8.
19. Southern Baptist Convention Bylaw 10.

20. Southern Baptist Convention Bylaw 11.
21. Southern Baptist Convention Constitution, Article V.
22. Southern Baptist Convention Bylaw 21.
23. Southern Baptist Convention Bylaw 17.
24. Southern Baptist Convention Bylaw 18.E.8.
25. Southern Baptist Convention Bylaw 18.
26. Ibid.
27. Southern Baptist Convention Constitution, Article X.
28. 2014–2015 Cooperative Program Allocation Budget, http://www
    .sbc.net/pdf/cp/2014–2015CPAllocationBudget.pdf.
29. 2010 Southern Baptist Convention *Annual*, 88.
30. 2011 Southern Baptist Convention *Annual*, 61–62.
31. *Southern Baptist Convention Organization Manual*, 3.
32. Ibid.
33. Ibid., 4.
34. Ibid.
35. "God's Plan for Sharing (GPS)," NAMB.net, https://www.namb
    .net/evangelism/gps; and "Send Relief Overview," NAMB.net,
    https://www.namb.net/send-relief.
36. *Southern Baptist Convention Organization Manual*, 5.
37. Ibid., 5–6.
38. Ibid., 10.
39. Ibid., 10.
40. Greg Wills, *Southern Baptist Theological Seminary, 1859–2000*
    (New York: Oxford University Press, 2009), 3–5.
41. Table 1.2, Association of Theological Schools 2015–2016 Annual
    Data Tables, https://www.ats.edu/uploads/resources/institutional
    -data/annual-data-tables/2015–2016-annual-data-tables.pdf.
42. *Southern Baptist Convention Organizational Manual*, 7.
43. Ibid.
44. Ibid., 9.
45. 1947 Southern Baptist Convention *Annual*, 33–34.
46. 1953 Southern Baptist Convention *Annual*, 53.
47. 1997 Southern Baptist Convention *Annual*, 74–79.
48. Ibid.
49. Ibid., 14.

50. Ibid.

51. Ibid.

52. Southern Baptist Convention Constitution, Article VI.

53. Southern Baptist Convention Bylaw 19.

54. Southern Baptist Convention Bylaw 15.

55. Southern Baptist Convention Bylaw 20.

56. Southern Baptist Convention Bylaw 8.

57. Southern Baptist Convention Bylaw 21.

58. "About Baptist Press," Baptist Press, htttp://www.bpnews.net, accessed June 29, 2017.

59. Southern Baptist Convention Bylaw 17.

60. Robert et al., *Robert's Rules of Order*, 27.

61. Chad Brand and David Hankins, *One Sacred Effort* (Nashville: B&H Academic, 2006), 101.

62. 2011 Southern Baptist Convention *Annual*, 137.

63. 2013 Southern Baptist Convention *Annual*, 126–27.

64. 1943 Southern Baptist Convention *Annual*, 21.

65. Southern Baptist Convention Bylaw 18.

66. Southern Baptist Convention Bylaw 30.

67. Thom Rainer, "A Resurgence Not Yet Realized: Evangelistic Effectiveness in the Southern Baptist Convention Since 1979," *Southern Baptist Journal of Theology* 9, no. 1 (Spring 2005): 55.

68. Thom Rainer, "A Plea for a More Civil Discourse," *Christian Post*, August 21, 2007.

69. Daniel L. Akin, "Axioms for a Great Commission Resurgence," sermon delivered April 16, 2009, Southeastern Baptist Theological Seminary.

70. 2009 Southern Baptist Convention *Annual*, 84.

71. http://www.sbc.net/aboutus/legal

72. http://www.sbc.net/aboutus/legal/constitution.asp

73. http://www.sbc.net/aboutus/legal/bylaws.asp

74. http://www.sbc.net/aboutus/legal/businessfinancialplan.asp

75. http://www.sbc.net/bfm2000/bfm2000.asp

76. http://media2.sbhla.org.s3.amazonaws.com/annuals/SBC_Annual _2010.pdf, 78–98.

77. Albert McClellan, *The Executive Committee of the Southern Baptist Convention* (Nashville: Broadman Press, 1985), 127.